Gu

VOL 20 / PART 1   2004

Edited by Jeremy Duff and Katharine Dell

Suggestions for using *Guidelines*

Set aside a regular time and place, if possible, when you can read and pray undisturbed. Before you begin, take time to be still and, if you find it helpful, use the BRF prayer.

In *Guidelines*, the introductory section provides context for the passages or themes to be studied, while the units of comment can be used daily, weekly, or whatever best fits your timetable. You will need a Bible (more than one if you want to compare different translations) as Bible passages are not included. At the end of each week is a 'Guidelines' section, offering further thoughts about, or practical application of what you have been studying.

You may find it helpful to keep a journal to record your thoughts about your study, or to note items for prayer. Another way of using *Guidelines* is to meet with others to discuss the material, either regularly or occasionally.

Occasionally, you may read something in *Guidelines* that you find particularly challenging, even uncomfortable. This is inevitable in a series of notes which draws on a wide spectrum of contributors, and doesn't believe in ducking difficult issues. Indeed, we believe that *Guidelines* readers much prefer thought-provoking material to a bland diet that only confirms what they already think.

If you do disagree with a contributor, you may find it helpful to go through these three steps. First, think about why you feel uncomfortable. Perhaps this is an idea that is new to you, or you are not happy at the way something has been expressed. Or there may be something more substantial—you may feel that the writer is guilty of sweeping generalization, factual error, theological or ethical misjudgment. Second, pray that God would use this disagreement to teach you more about his word and about yourself. Third, think about what you will do as a result of the disagreement. You might resolve to find out more about the issue, or write to the contributor or the editors of *Guidelines*. After all, we aim to be 'doers of the word', not just people who hold opinions about it.

Writers in this issue

Graham Tomlin is Vice Principal and tutor in Historical Theology and Evangelism at Wycliffe Hall, Oxford, from where he leads many parish evangelistic mission events. Formerly he was a curate in Exeter, and a college chaplain. His most recent books include *The Provocative Church* (SPCK, 2002) and *Luther and his World* (Lion, 2002).

Trevor Dennis is well known to *Guidelines* readers for his stimulating contributions. Now Canon Chancellor of Chester Cathedral, he was formerly Vice Principal of Salisbury and Wells Theological College. His books include *Lo and Behold! The Power of Old Testament Storytelling* and *Sarah Laughed*.

Andrew Atherstone is the curate of Christ Church, Abingdon. He is also an expert in 19th-century church history—why the Church of England has turned out as it is!

Joanna McGrath is a consultant clinical psychologist specializing in brain injury and neurological rehabilitation. She has a particular interest in the Gospels, and making connections between psychology and the Bible. She is the co-author of *Self-Esteem* (IVP, 2002).

John Day is Reader in Biblical Studies in the University of Oxford and Fellow and Tutor of Lady Margaret Hall, Oxford.

John Parr is an Anglican priest. After working in parish and diocesan posts, and on the staff of a theological college, he is now a mental health advocate in Suffolk. He continues to be involved in ordination training.

Paula Gooder teaches Biblical Studies, both Old and New Testament, at the Queen's Ecumenical Theological Foundation, Birmingham, as well as working freelance as a Biblical Studies writer and lecturer. She has recently published *The Pentateuch: A Story of Beginnings* (Continuum, 2000) and is currently working on a commentary on 2 Corinthians for the Blackwells commentary series.

Further BRF reading for this issue

For more in-depth coverage of some of the passages in these
Bible reading notes, we recommend the following titles:

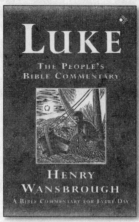

LUKE
THE PEOPLE'S BIBLE COMMENTARY

HENRY
WANSBROUGH

A BIBLE COMMENTARY FOR EVERY DAY

1 84101 027 8, £7.99

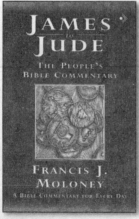

JAMES to JUDE
THE PEOPLE'S BIBLE COMMENTARY

FRANCIS J.
MOLONEY

A BIBLE COMMENTARY FOR EVERY DAY

1 84101 092 8, £7.99

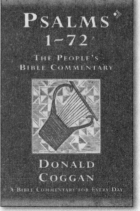

PSALMS 1–72
THE PEOPLE'S BIBLE COMMENTARY

DONALD
COGGAN

A BIBLE COMMENTARY FOR EVERY DAY

1 84101 031 6, £7.99

The Editors write...

Transformation is a key issue in life—do our lives continue for ever the same? This strikes us particularly at this time of year, running from New Year's Day to April when the creation around us is blooming into its new life. It also contains Easter—the point in the Christian year which proclaims most strongly that transformation is possible.

Guidelines is certainly not standing still. We have to say goodbye and thank you to John Parr, who, for the last ten years, has been one of our joint editors. It is fitting that in this issue John finishes his series on the writings of Luke, bringing us to Easter and the transformation of the resurrection. Jeremy Duff is the new joint editor to work alongside Katharine. Jeremy is a tutor in New Testament at Wycliffe Hall in Oxford, although he lives in his home town of Liverpool where his wife Jill is a minister in a deprived area of the city.

We start the new year with Graham Tomlin challenging us to think about church—what is it for? We then have a lively contribution from Trevor Dennis, one of our regular contributors, on Genesis 25—33. This is in response to a reader's letter which pointed out that, while other parts of Genesis have been well covered over the years, this section has been somewhat neglected. We do listen to your requests!

Andrew Atherstone is then our guide through the letters of John, with their twin focus on truth and love. Next, Joanna McGrath, a consultant clinical psychologist, leads us 'through paradox to transformation', exploring how people change in the New Testament. We then continue our coverage of the Psalms by looking at 'Book 2', Psalms 42—72, with a contribution from a well-known Psalms scholar, John Day.

After John Parr's inspiring conclusion to the writings of Luke, we close with our fifth new contributor, Paula Gooder, who gives us some fascinating insights into the second part of Isaiah (chs. 40 to 55), looking at the vision of hope for the exiles that this section of the book brings—the transformation to which they looked forward.

Katharine Dell, Jeremy Duff
Joint Editors

The BRF Prayer

Almighty God,
you have taught us that your word is a lamp for our
feet and a light for our path. Help us, and all who
prayerfully read your word, to deepen our
fellowship with each other through your love. And
in so doing may we come to know you more fully,
love you more truly, and follow more faithfully in
the steps of your son Jesus Christ, who lives and
reigns with you and the Holy Spirit,
one God for evermore. Amen.

THE PROVOCATIVE CHURCH

The decline of the Church in the West is well known and well documented. Figures appear regularly, telling us that the Church is in serious, perhaps even terminal, decline. The former Archbishop of Canterbury, George Carey, has said that in its traditional heartlands of western Europe, the Church is slowly 'bleeding to death'. At the same time, many Christians feel that traditional methods of evangelism are both inappropriate and ineffective in the new post-modern culture that surrounds us. These notes encourage us to look at what the New Testament says about evangelism with new eyes, to see how churches might be turned around to become the kind of places that can attract and hold those who at present have no time for church at all. They use the New Revised Standard Version (NRSV).

1 What does all this mean?

Acts 2:1–13

On the day of Pentecost, Jerusalem is buzzing with the languages, dress and customs of the Jewish diaspora, staying in the city for the Feast of Weeks. Suddenly a group of people break out of a house, worshipping God exuberantly and excitedly. In the middle of the noise and confusion, a man stands up among them to announce a radical new message, to offer an entirely new angle on the history of Israel, claiming that its climax has now come in the recent events in the city, which had led to the death and mysterious resurrection of Jesus of Nazareth.

Whichever way you look at it, Peter's sermon is remarkable. Luke, the author of Acts, tells us that as a result, three thousand people joined this new sect who saw themselves as followers of Jesus (2:41). Yet what was it that led to such fascination with the message? Clearly it wasn't Peter's eloquence or learning. Instead it was the remarkable and sudden ability of these rural Galilean followers of Jesus to praise God in all the different languages of the diaspora (vv. 7–8). The key comes in verse 12: 'Amazed and perplexed', they asked each other, 'What does this mean?' The people who heard Peter were first of all intrigued by what they had seen—something they could not easily explain, and which posed a question, which in turn demanded an answer. Busy crowds, hurrying to the temple or simply going about their normal business, were stopped in their tracks as the rumour spread that uneducated Galileans were speaking languages rarely heard among the natives of the capital city.

Evangelism is most effective when it follows in the wake of something remarkable. The gospel is best proclaimed when there is already an audience of people who are eager to know. The best evangelism happens when people have encountered something extraordinary in the life of a Christian or a church community, something that makes them ask the simple question, 'What does all this mean?' What remarkable happenings in our churches might make our contemporaries ask, 'What does this all mean?' It might not be a surprising, miraculous facility with languages, but it may be an unexpected compassion, an unusual sacrifice, or an answered prayer for healing, which provides the occasion for evangelism that really works.

2 Provoking questions

1 Peter 3:8–18

This brief letter, written from Rome to churches in Asia Minor (modern-day Turkey), has as its major theme the way Christians are to behave and speak within a wider non-Christian society. As one writer puts it, this is 'the New Testament document that most vigorously united the witness of the word with the witness of Christian presence in society' (L. Goppelt, *Theology of the New Testament Vol II*, Eerdmans, p. 178). In today's passage, it is significant that Peter doesn't offer evangelism as the primary way in which the believers are to relate to non-Christians. First and foremost comes the quality of life within the Christian community. Here, people are meant to find harmony, sympathy, love, compassion and humility. These churches are urged to give careful attention to how these qualities can be expressed, and grow, in their own lives. Alongside this, in their relations with surrounding pagans, the Christians are to ensure that their lives are tinged with such practical goodness that, despite the common suspicions of Christian malpractice or irrelevance, their non-Christian neighbours cannot help acknowledging that God makes a difference in a human life (2:12).

The whole approach is summed up in verse 15. The priority for Christians seeking to live in a non-Christian society is this: 'In your hearts, sanctify Christ as Lord.' These Christian communities are to bring the whole of their lives increasingly under the gentle and strong rule of Christ. They are to allow that rule to shape everything, such as the value they place on their possessions (1:18), their role as citizens and subjects (2:13–17), the way a victimized worker might relate to her employer (2:18–25) and the way their marriages work (3:1–8). As they begin to work out what living under the rule of Christ means and to put it into practice, then they might begin to find that friends and family members start to ask questions, perhaps about 'the hope that is in them' (v. 15). Then they are to be ready with an answer.

Such a strategy has much to offer us in similar circumstances, surrounded by an increasingly non-Christian culture. Christians do need to be able to speak sensibly about why they believe; yet such evangelism works best when it is the answer to a question already raised. How might you provoke such a question today?

3 Words and deeds

Luke 7:11–23

This is a truly astonishing story. Jesus and his friends, entering a small Galilean town, bump into a funeral procession. We might have expected a few words of comfort to the family, an expression of sorrow at their loss. Yet, gripped with compassion at the despair of the grieving mother, Jesus ignores her and instead addresses the corpse. The dead man slowly begins to stir, rises from the bier, and then even starts to speak. It's not surprising that 'fear seized all of them' (v. 16)!

At this point in the story, Luke introduces the disciples of John the

Baptist. They come wondering whether this prophet really is the one whom all Israel is waiting for. Jesus' reply is intriguing. He does not claim the title of Son of God, or even Messiah. He simply points the messengers to his actions, the remarkable things that keep on happening around him, and invites them to think about the significance of these deeds. Passages such as Isaiah 29:18–19 and 35:5–6 lie very clearly in the background. Of course Jesus is the one Israel has been waiting for, but this is not just because he claims to be the one, but because through him the signs that indicate the coming of God to rescue his people are present.

Sometimes, Jesus is presented as primarily a teacher of wise things, with the miracles portrayed just as naïve stories that get in the way of his true spiritual message. Nothing could be further from the truth. The identity of Jesus as the expected one is found not in his words, but in his deeds. In fact, his words act like commentaries on his deeds, explaining their meaning: we're reminded of Jesus' words to the crowds later in Luke's Gospel, 'If it is by the finger of God that I cast out the demons, then the kingdom of God has come to you' (Luke 11:20). Perhaps one of the reasons why the church is failing in the West is that, very often, our words are hollow. In other words, we have no reality to point to, no integrity between our words and actions. Just as Jesus' words were a commentary on his remarkable deeds, the Church's evangelism, its words of invitation to come to believe in Christ, are meant to be commentaries, explanations of the remarkable things that happen in a community of people truly open to the working of the Spirit of God.

4 The divine exhibition

Ephesians 3:2–11

In this passage, Paul's vision of the gospel is laid out. It is breathtaking and not a little surprising. He has already explained his understanding of God's plan for the future—a world where all of fractured creation is brought back together, healed and restored under God's rule in Christ (1:10). Yet his description of the heart of his message is not what we might expect. For him, the central 'mystery' of the gospel is that now

Gentiles are welcome alongside Jewish believers among God's people (v. 6). The 'plan of the mystery hidden for ages in God who created all things' (v. 9) has now been revealed, and it comprises this coming together of both Jew and Gentile within God's people. A crucial stage in God's plan has been reached, and Paul describes how God now intends to show off his wisdom and craft to the rest of the cosmos (v. 10). God the divine artist wants to hold an exhibition of such beauty and power and wisdom that anyone who looks on, whether they come from earth or heaven, will be overcome with awe. It is to be a display of his 'manifold (the word can be otherwise translated as 'varied' or 'variegated') wisdom'. And this is where the Jew/Gentile issue comes in. For Paul, the hard evidence that God will one day bring all things together under Christ is found in these small Christian communities scattered around the Roman empire, which are busy uniting Gentile and Jew, freemen and slaves, women and men, sitting alongside one another, sharing the same bread and wine in cities across the Roman empire. This is, if you like, the sneak preview of the exhibition, the trailer for the main feature yet to be shown.

Christian unity (not the dry, institutional, paper kind, but the warm, supportive, personal kind) has a key role to play in evangelism. A community where you find social and racial differences transcended, where very different people from very different backgrounds somehow learn to care for each other and enjoy their diversity, a community where all kinds of people can learn the simple yet so difficult art of loving, as they gradually grasp how much they are loved by their creator, is a profoundly attractive place. It will find people wanting to join up without its having to try too hard.

5 Staying loyal to the true king

Matthew 28:16–20

These last few verses of Matthew's Gospel are famous for their description of the 'great commission' which Jesus left for his followers to fulfil. Jesus is surrounded by a crowd where faith, doubt and worship are all mixed up together (v. 17). Yet despite this, he gives them an inspiring vision for the rest of their lives. Verse 18 directly echoes Daniel 7:14, which spoke of Israel's hope that, one day, all the nations would come to serve and worship the one true God. The point being made is clear. The resurrected Jesus is the one to whom all authority on heaven and earth is given. He is the 'Son of Man', the rightful ruler of heaven and earth, the one who rules in God's name, not just over Israel but over the Gentile world as well—and the task of this small band of his followers is to announce that rule to the whole of creation.

The legend of Robin Hood is better known than its supposed historical context. In the 12th century, the rightful king, Richard, left England to fight in the Crusades and, in his absence, his cruel and oppressive brother Prince John set himself up as king in his place. Robin Hood was the leader of a kind of resistance movement which refused to accept the rule of 'king' John, and kept alive the hope of the return of the true king. Robin Hood's band of resistance fighters is a surprising but not inappropriate image for the Church in the world today. Christians too live under a regime where oppression and injustice seem to be in charge, but they can laugh merrily because they know that the present system is not the last word. They know that the true king is coming, and that things will one day be different. From time to time, they still remind the false powers that their rule is temporary and bogus, by acts of rebellion which remember the true king. They also whisper around the good news that things don't have to be like this.

This is essentially what evangelism is—the simple announcement that there is another king, another kingdom, that will one day become fully visible, and the invitation to take part in that kingdom. The reign of evil, sin and death is temporary and its days are numbered. This is why Christians evangelize, even under the apparently hostile conditions of post-modernity.

6 Evangelism for the terrified

Colossians 4:2–6

Many Christians struggle with the idea of evangelism because they know they are not evangelists. Perhaps you've watched another

Christian across the room at a party, who is clearly gifted in this area, talking naturally and freely about his or her faith, while you know that whenever the subject comes up, you get tongue-tied, embarrassed and inexplicably incoherent. It perhaps comes as a relief, then, to realize that the New Testament has a place for everyone in the task of evangelism, and it doesn't involve all of us becoming experts at answering difficult philosophical questions, or persuading people into faith. In this brief passage, Paul addresses the local Christians in Colossae about their responsibilities towards 'outsiders', while at the same time defining his own responsibilities as an evangelist. He seems to highlight two major responsibilities in particular for 'ordinary' Christians, and neither involves a degree in theology.

They are firstly to 'devote (them)selves to prayer' (v. 2), paying close attention to God, day in, day out, and ensuring that such prayer is heavily laced with gratitude. In addition to a life rooted in prayer, they are to 'conduct (them)selves wisely towards outsiders' (v. 5). The disciples of Jesus are not to live in a holy huddle of the pure—they are to live *public* Christian lives, actively building positive relationships with those outside the faith. And they are to 'act wisely', conducting their lives in a way that breathes the wisdom that comes from a life of prayer and close attention to God and the scriptures. This wisdom comes to a focus in their speech, which has to be 'gracious', extending a warm, non-judgmental, welcoming kindness, yet at the same time 'seasoned with salt', never apologizing for being a Christian, making no secret of their Christian activity and commitment (v. 6).

Alongside this, there is the task of the evangelist. Paul sees it as his task to 'declare the mystery of Christ… reveal(ing) it clearly as I should' (vv. 3–4). Not every Christian is gifted at doing this, but some are. Most growing churches now have courses such as Alpha, which provide a setting where the questions raised by Christian lives lived in the world can be answered, and where those with evangelistic gifts can explain the meaning of the faith. When the lived witness of public Christian lives comes together with the skilled, explanatory words of the evangelist, then so often we find that God 'opens a door for the word' in the lives of those who both watch and listen.

Guidelines

A provocative lifestyle that makes Christian faith intriguing and attractive will have deep roots in a life of prayer. Pray for:

- Increasing intimacy with God as each week passes.
- The peace of a heart and mind fixed on God, which will stand out as distinctive in a stressed and busy world.
- Two friends, neighbours or family members whose lives you long to see come under the gentle and wise rule of Christ.
- Your local church, that it may reflect the values of Christ's kingdom in its life, relationships and compassionate ministry to people in its area.

God and Father, you loved the world so much that you gave your only Son for the salvation of humankind. Help your Church to be a light in the darkness, a city on a hill, a place where people everywhere can find the grace, mercy and love of the God who made them. Keep me mindful this day that I live my life under the rule of Christ, and may my life provoke questions in the minds of those around me, that they may see the difference you make in a human life. May I be ready with a word of wisdom for all who seek you. Through Jesus Christ your Son, Amen.

FURTHER READING

William J. Abraham, *The Logic of Evangelism* (Hodder, 1989)

John Drane, *Faith in a Changing Culture* (Marshall Pickering, 1997)

Graham Tomlin, *The Provocative Church* (SPCK, 2002)

Robert Warren, *Being Human, Being Church* (Marshall Pickering, 1995)

GENESIS 25—33

These chapters tell the story of Jacob and Esau. From the end of chapter 11 to the first part of chapter 25, Genesis is largely concerned with Abraham, the promises of God, and the lack of a son on whom the fulfilment of those promises depend. When finally this son, Isaac, is born, he is on stage for a remarkably short time. He is the central character in chapter 26, and plays a large part in 27, but by then his sons Jacob and Esau have been born and are ready to take over the story. At least, Jacob is: he seizes it by the scruff of the neck!

The stories we will be looking at these next two weeks are stories of struggle—between Isaac and his wife Rebekah, between Jacob and his uncle Laban, between Jacob's two wives, Leah and Rachel, between Jacob and God, and above all between Jacob and Esau. They include some of the most moving stories in the Bible, as well as some of the most hilarious, and two of its most profound tales of encounter with God. They will end in chapter 33 with a story of unexpected reconciliation and a forgiveness which is so remarkable that Jacob cannot quite take it in.

We will only have time to cover the more significant stories. In preparing these notes, I have used the NRSV, but for your own study any reputable translation will do.

Genesis 25:19—29:14

1 The struggle begins

Genesis 25:19–34

God gives himself a hard time in Genesis. He has plans for the creation of his own people. For those plans to come to anything, the ancestors of that people must have children, and, indeed, sons. However, God keeps choosing couples who have problems conceiving. In the case of Abraham and Sarah, those difficulties are first introduced at 11:30 and not solved till 21:2, when Isaac is born. In 25:21 we are told that Isaac's wife, Rebekah, is also barren, and at 25:26 we learn that they waited *twenty years* for a child! But the storyteller is not concerned with the pain of their waiting. The 'child' turns out to be twin boys, and it is their struggle with one another that he wants to tell us about. It will provide his main theme till the end of chapter 33.

The struggle begins while the twins are still embryos. They fight so much in her womb that Rebekah can scarcely endure it. She turns to God in prayer. God provides some clarity, but hardly reassurance. He explains that the fighting will continue, that the younger of the two boys will get the better of the older one, and that their struggles will mirror the later historical conflicts between Israel and the people of Edom to the south-east (Esau is to be the ancestor of the Edomites, while the people of Israel will be descended from Jacob).

Jacob is born grasping Esau's heel. Already he is attempting to hold Esau back, trying to get there first. He does not succeed at that point, but once he and his brother are grown up, it seems he gets his way all too easily. Esau trades in his birthright, all the considerable privileges of the elder son, for a bowl of lentils!

We have to be alert to the prejudice that hides in this episode and its portrayal of Esau, the ancestor of the Edomites—prejudice against the hunter-gatherer, who can only think of his stomach, and contempt for the Edomite people. Still in our world hunter-gatherers are often despised, and whole peoples are stereotyped as uncivilized or inadequate. We need to be aware of the prejudice around us and within us—and acknowledging this where it occurs in the Bible will help us do that.

2 A cruel trick

Genesis 27:1–20

In Genesis 25:28, we learn that 'Isaac loved Esau… but Rebekah loved Jacob'. So to the struggle between the brothers is added the struggle between their parents. It is only hinted at there, but in chapter 27 it spills out on to the page in deceit and humiliation.

Isaac is very vulnerable. We learn that immediately, in verse 1. He is blind and weak and approaching death. Before he dies, he must bless the son who will take his place as head of the family. The solemn moment of that blessing will be one of the most significant in his whole life, and will be done in the presence of God (see v. 7). Indeed, the power of the blessing will come from God, from whom all blessing flows and all true empowerment comes.

But Isaac makes a mistake. His deathbed blessing will confer more than status within the family. The promises of God are at stake, the promises delivered first to Abraham and then to Isaac himself in 26:3–5. Isaac knows full well that those promises cannot be inherited by more than one of his sons. Did not his own half-brother, Ishmael, have to be banished into the desert in chapter 21? But he chooses the wrong son. He chooses Esau because he is the older of the two, and because Esau is a hunter like him. He allows human convention and his own favouritism to get the better of him. He forgets that, with God, the last are first and the first last.

Yet this story is not hard on Jacob. He is most cruelly deceived, and by his own wife and one of his sons. The strongest character is Rebekah. She is the one who overhears the vital conversation between Isaac and Esau, who knows exactly what to do at every turn, and spurs a cautious Jacob into action. In doing so, she serves the declared purposes of God. Yet in the process she destroys her relationship with her husband, makes her sons into enemies of one another, and brings Jacob's innate trickery to a terrible flowering, to the point where he answers his father's question about how he found his game so quickly by saying, 'Because the Lord your God granted me success' (v. 20). A bit rich, that!

Rebekah and Jacob should have been more patient, we say. They should have waited for God. Yet Isaac is *dying* here, and he must bless Jacob before he does. There is no time for Rebekah and Jacob to wait. Is God, then, the true villain of this piece, that he should put human beings in the position of having to behave so cruelly to advance his purposes? Is not a God who chooses one and rejects another bound to cause conflict and pain? Do we believe that God ever chooses one and rejects another?

The Bible has a habit of raising hard questions.

3 Cries of pain

In the little story of the lentil soup, it seemed that Esau was dismissed as impossibly stupid, caring only for his stomach and the clamouring needs of the moment. We saw him there through the lens of stereotype. Yet there is no prejudice here in chapter 27. Esau may not be the one chosen to be the bearer of the promises of God, and yet the storyteller goes out of his way to let us hear his pain, as well as the distress of his father.

Jacob, after moments of agonizing suspense, gains his blessing. He has got what he came for, and at once leaves his father's tent. Almost immediately Esau takes his place, to be greeted with the unexpected and unnerving question from his father, 'Who are you?' 'I am your firstborn son, Esau,' Esau replies. That is what Jacob answered when he came into the tent, but his voice did not convince, and Isaac needed further evidence. Now he needs none. The voice is too familiar, his love for Esau too strong. So the truth comes out, and we hear Esau's heart-rending cry, 'Bless me, me also, father!' Yet in this world of Genesis, where one son receives so much more than another—the world of so much of the Bible, where God chooses one and rejects another—there is not enough blessing to go round. Isaac does respond to Esau's second howling plea with fine poetry, but the lines are more curse than blessing, until we reach the last one: 'you shall break [your brother's] yoke from your neck' (v. 40).

What will that mean? Violence? Bloodshed? Or forgiveness? We shall see. The story will surprise us.

4 Farewell, or flight?

The beginning of this passage encourages us to fear the worst. Esau, who once acted in such ill-considered haste when he accepted Jacob's offer of a bowl of soup, is now prepared to wait. He will wait for Isaac to die, and then he will lie in wait for his brother. It will all soon be over, he supposes. He is wrong. He will have to wait twenty years for a conclusion, and when it comes it will be quite different from the one he envisages.

In Esau's world, vengeance is a moral duty. When a man has been disgraced by another, he must recover his honour by taking vengeance. 'An eye for an eye, and a tooth for a tooth,' Exodus 21:24 famously says. It takes it for granted that people will try to avenge themselves, but seeks to put a limit on their actions: an eye, *and no more than an eye*, for an eye; a tooth, *and no more than a tooth*, for a tooth. In Esau's case, not only he, but his dying father also, has been treated with contempt. 'Honour your father and mother.' That too is in Exodus (20:12). Esau must kill his brother to restore Isaac's honour, as well as his own.

Yet vengeance only adds violence to violence, and wreaks still more havoc. We are not the only ones to understand that. Rebekah knows it very well, and so she comes up with another plan to get Jacob out of harm's way—a brilliant plan, for must not God's promise-bearer marry within the family, and avoid taking a foreign wife? Did not Abraham forbid the idea of Isaac marrying a Canaanite woman and send his servant to fetch Rebekah herself from Paddan-aram, she a daughter of one of his nephews (see 24:1–4, 23–27)?

Isaac falls for this plan, too. Unlike Rebekah, he seems unaware of the hatred that is tearing his family apart, and to have forgotten Jacob's humiliation of him. He sends Jacob away to Paddan-aram with words of another blessing ringing in his ears (28:2–4), words which remind us clearly of the promises that God once made to Abraham and to Isaac himself.

Are they the words of an old man who has retreated into the past, to get away from the pain and terror that surround him? Or do they mean that the story is firmly back on track and the promises of God are once more in their rightful place? The storyteller does not answer that, but meanwhile we know that Jacob will not be able to return immediately he has found a wife. He will need to wait until Rebekah sends him word that it is safe to come back. But when will that be? For the time being, Jacob must carry the promises of God into exile.

God, of course, is used to being in exile.

5 A stairway to heaven

Genesis 28:10–22

As he leaves what one day will be the promised land—and, four chapters later, as he returns to it and crosses the river Jabbok—Jacob meets God. Of all the Bible's stories of encounter with God, these two are among the most remarkable.

Jacob is extremely vulnerable here: he has a long journey ahead of him, to an uncertain conclusion, and a murderous brother behind him. He has nothing with him but words of blessing, which seem now to count for nothing. It has all gone wrong. By his own reckoning, he will have to rely on God even for his 'bread to eat and clothing to wear' (v. 20).

Suddenly, against all expectations, this Jacob finds himself on the edge of heaven, a heaven whose door is wide open, a heaven linked to his patch of ground by a great stairway (that's a better translation than 'ladder'). He does not need to climb the stairs to reach it, for God's messengers come down to him, and then God himself stands beside him. A down-to-earth God! And a God with words of blessing in his mouth, words that confirm the blessing that Isaac gave him before he left home, words that include those that we all wish to hear, words that go to the heart of our deepest longings: 'Know that I am with you and will keep you… I will bring you back… I will not leave you' (v. 15).

What was, when Jacob lay down to sleep, an ordinary place of no significance (whoever has heard of Luz?) is now Beth El (Hebrew for the house of God), the very gate of heaven. He wakes and knows it was not just a dream. 'Surely the Lord is in this place!' he cries. He is surrounded by God and is overwhelmed, as well he might be—until, that is, religious ritual brings him back towards his old ways and he starts bargaining (vv. 20–22)!

But what about Isaac and Esau? Whose side is this God on? The side of the trickster, the one who deceives and humiliates? It would seem so, at least for the present. This passage is magnificent, but also appears deeply flawed. God is both revealed and hidden here.

6 A homecoming?

Genesis 29:1–14

In Genesis 24 there was another meeting by this well. Abraham's servant, laden with gold, jewellery and fine garments, and trailing camels, came there to find a wife for Isaac. Rebekah arrived with her water jar, and he discovered that she was Abraham's great-niece. She ran home with the news about him, and her brother Laban then ran out to meet him. The servant explained his purpose and saw the hand of God in it all. The gifts were handed over, and the servant departed to return to Isaac, bringing Rebekah with him.

In this much shorter passage in chapter 29, history nearly repeats itself. This time Laban's own daughter Rachel arrives at the well, not with a water jar, but with a flock of her father's sheep. Jacob discovers before she reaches the well who she is. She is family! And when he tells her so, she runs off to tell Laban, just as Rebekah did, and Laban runs out to meet him, just as he did before, and welcomes him into his home.

Yet there are differences, also, beyond the absence of the water jar. When Abraham's servant set eyes on Rebekah, his interest was in her family, her beauty and her virginity. He wished to be sure she was a suitable bride for Isaac. When Jacob meets Rachel, the sheep come first (v. 10)! Only once he has watered the animals does he kiss Rachel, and then not as a lover, but as kinsman.

There is another difference, too. Jacob has no gold, silver, fine cloth or camels with him. He has nothing to give Laban. Verse 14 is not such an enthusiastic greeting as our English translations make it sound. 'Oh well, you're family. I suppose you'd better stay a while' is more the sense of it.

Jacob may weep with relief and happiness, glad to be among his own kith and kin. But he is not going to find it as easy as Abraham's servant did. Too right he isn't!

Guidelines

We must not let the fact that these stories are in the Bible prevent us from *enjoying* them! They are told with consummate skill and are designed to entertain. Though our own society may be different in so many ways, we can engage with these stories with ease, for the humanity of the characters and the nature of so much of their predicament are so familiar.

Yet the air these stories breathe is sacred. God lies behind every one of them, though he only comes out into the open at Beth El. With this God, the last are first and the first last. He stands by the sinner and fills the ear with words of blessing. That is good and speaks of the God we find in Christ. And yet, as we have discovered, not all the characters in these stories benefit from God's presence. Some suffer because of him, and most grievously so. Esau for one, and Isaac (even Isaac!) for another. That surely cannot be right.

Still to this day, millions suffer because of what some people believe and say about God. Many find themselves humiliated, excluded, rejected by Christians. Does anyone suffer because of our beliefs? It is a hard question to face, but for other people's sake, and for God's sake, we must ask it.

Genesis 29:15—33:17

1 Rachel and Leah

Genesis 29:15–30

Jacob the trickster gets his come-uppance here—for his uncle Laban is a trickster, too, and a clever one at that. Laban's offer at the start of this passage may sound like generosity—it is meant to—but he is actually treating Jacob no longer as a member of the family, but as one of his workers. His terms are harsh, also. *Seven years* for Rachel! Never mind what Jacob feels them to be, seven years is a very long time to wait.

But Laban has another trick up his sleeve. He puts the wrong woman in Jacob's bed on his wedding night, and when Jacob protests the next morning, he replies, 'Oh, didn't you know? We always marry off the older daughters first.' To that, Jacob is speechless, though we might well have thought he would say, 'Why in heaven's name didn't you tell me that seven years ago?'

It is all great fun, especially when we start speculating on how Laban managed it. He must have got Jacob blind drunk at the wedding feast, say the rabbis!

But what about Rachel and Leah? Their father uses them to get as much out of Jacob as he can. They are treated as commodities to be traded for work in Laban's fields. And what of the fateful day of the wedding? Are the two women in on the plan? The story does not say so. They seem to have no power at all. So we imagine Rachel sitting through what she thinks is her wedding feast, only to be shoved aside by her father at the last moment and replaced by her sister. And Leah, we presume, also knows nothing until she is bundled into the tent of a man who does not love her. Did it feel like rape that night? Did she lie there in the dark, frightened to death of what Jacob might do to her in the morning when he discovered who she was?

All the stories, poems and letters in the Bible are written from particular points of view—not God's, as if the passages descended pure and unsullied from heaven, but almost invariably those of men. Just as we must recognize racism when we find it in the Bible, so must we acknowledge its sexism.

2 Jacob and Laban

Genesis 30:25–43

No word has come from Rebekah to say that it is safe for Jacob to return home. But once a son is born to his beloved Rachel, he decides it is time to go. In Exodus 5:1, Moses and Aaron will confront a tyrannical pharaoh with the words, 'Thus says the Lord... "Let my people go"', and the pharaoh will reply, 'Who is the Lord, that I should heed him and let Israel go?' Laban is not a tyrant, but in some ways he is harder to deal with. At least the pharaoh will speak plainly, and Moses and Aaron will know where they stand. Laban coats his words in honey, and Jacob puts them in his mouth before he realizes how bitter they are. 'Name your wages,' Laban says. What generosity! Until we remember that the word 'wages' underlines Jacob's status as one of his uncle's workers, robbed of his belonging to the family; until we catch the hint that Laban wants more work out of Jacob, and is in effect refusing to let him go home.

Yet Jacob thinks he has the measure of him this time. He presents Laban with a plan he cannot refuse: Jacob will only take the sheep and goats which are unusually marked or coloured. But see already how Laban's words have seduced him! He is no longer talking of going home, but of setting up on his own. How much longer will it be before he is free of Laban?

Meanwhile, Laban means to keep Jacob in poverty and dependent on him. He removes all the speckled and spotted goats and the black lambs, the ones he has just agreed Jacob can have, and takes them three days' journey away. This time he has made a mistake. He under-estimates Jacob's skills as a stock-breeder and, by leaving him on his own, he gives him the opportunity to put them to good effect. Jacob's methods are strange indeed to our ears. He seems to believe that the markings and colour of goats and sheep are determined by what their parents can see at the time they mate! Yet it works, and Jacob for the first time becomes rich.

At Beth El, God promised Jacob that he would keep him wherever he went (see 28:15). It seems that he is fulfilling that promise. Will he keep his other promise to bring him back to Canaan?

3 The best trick of all

Genesis 31:17–35

We had thought there were two tricksters in these stories. Now we find that there is a third—Rachel.

Finally, after twenty years slaving for Laban, Jacob is told by God to return home. 'I will be with you,' says God, repeating words he first spoke at Beth El (see 31:3 and 28:15). So Jacob and his family escape. Laban is three days' journey away and knows nothing of their depart-ure. Yet inevitably he finds out and sets off in pursuit, as one day the pharaoh will pursue the Israelites fleeing from his brutal slavery in Exodus 14. Laban wants to get his hands on Jacob, his daughters, all those animals Jacob has… and his household gods!

Immediately before this passage, Rachel and Leah reveal how angry they are with their father. Feeling disowned by him, they break with him and his family. They belong entirely with Jacob now. And that, Rachel thinks, is where the family's household gods belong also. She wants for herself and her children the prosperity and the blessing she hopes they will bring. In Laban's hands they brought her nothing.

For Laban, their disappearance is a most serious matter, as he shows in his speech in verses 26–30. His words to Jacob are a mixture of rage, sweetness, hypocrisy, threat, resignation, bluster, and an acknowledgment of his powerlessness before a man who has God on his side. But his mention of his gods at the very end reveals why he has chased Jacob such a long way. That accusation surprises Jacob. Rachel has not told him what she has done. Full of moral outrage, Jacob makes the fearful promise that if anyone in his company is found with the gods, they shall die.

So, while we bite our nails, Laban ransacks the tents, and finally enters Rachel's. The game is up! But no. Rachel is the cleverest trickster of the lot. The gods are small figurines or masks and she is sitting on them, but she tells Laban that she cannot get up because she is in the middle of her period! There is an earthy Israelite humour at work here: an 'unclean' woman is sitting on 'unclean' idols and makes a fool out of a man so fiercely devoted to them! It is one of the great comic moments in the Bible.

After this passage there is more anger from Jacob, but in the end he and Laban make their peace with one another. Conflict is avoided and Jacob and his family continue on their way. Laban never does get his gods back!

4 Prayer and presents

Genesis 32:1–21

Still no word has come from Rebekah. Before Jacob left Canaan, she had told him she would send a messenger to him once Esau's anger had subsided. None has arrived. As far as Jacob knows, Esau is still minded to kill him. Messengers from God meet him and he stumbles upon God's camp, as he stumbled upon God's house at Beth El, but this does not reassure him. Is God encamped for war? Does that mean conflict between him and his brother? If so, whose side will God be on? As Jacob will soon acknowledge in prayer, he is not worthy of God's support.

At Beth El, God spoke. At Mahanaim, he is silent. Jacob's questions hang unanswered. So he must take things into his own hands. He sends his own messengers to Esau with hints of peace offerings to come, and hopes of reconciliation. Significantly, he refers to Esau as his 'lord', and to himself as his brother's 'servant'. Before the brothers were born, God told their mother, 'The elder shall serve the younger.' 'Be lord over your brothers,' Isaac declared when he blessed Jacob, 'and may your mother's sons bow down to you.' Jacob's years of exile with Laban have knocked all that for six. The old promise of God and the blessing of Isaac seem now to count for nothing. They seem to count for even less when the messengers return with the news that Esau is coming to meet him with *four hundred men*. That sounds like war, and Jacob assumes that it is.

Fearing imminent attack, he takes the desperate measure of dividing his company into two. He is prepared to sacrifice half of all he has, half of the people with him. But then, for the first time in these stories, he turns to God in prayer. 'I am too small,' he says (in a literal translation of the Hebrew of verse 10), 'for all you have done for me… Deliver me… for I am afraid.' There is none of Jacob's old trickery here, only honesty and humility. In recognizing his smallness, Jacob seems to be growing up.

Yet then the old Jacob reasserts himself. If prayer does not work, bribery might! A new plan is now put into action, more confident than the last. He will not wait for Esau to attack. He will overwhelm him with animals, so that he can hardly move! He will buy him off, and though before he was always trying to get ahead of his brother, this time he will willingly bring up the rear.

But what of reconciliation? If that is to be gained, it seems it will be up to Esau to offer it. And Esau is coming with four hundred men.

5 Wrestling with God

Jacob has reached his Rubicon. After this, there will be no going back.

So which way is he facing, once he has crossed his little company over the river? He has held back and is on his own. Is he about to turn and run? We do not know, but we are not left wondering for long, for suddenly, without warning, he finds himself wrestling with 'a man'.

Who is this mysterious stranger? Surely, we say, it must be Esau, come ahead of his army to find Jacob and kill him, or at least one of Esau's soldiers.

As the wrestling bout continues through the long dark hours, it becomes more and more mysterious. Jacob's hip is dislocated by a mere touch ('struck' in verse 25 is too strong a translation of the Hebrew). Yet he does not curl up in agony, as we might expect, but still seems to have the better of it. 'The man' begs to be released. 'Not unless you bless me!' cries Jacob. That is the old Jacob speaking, the Jacob who always wanted to be first, who wrestled with his brother at birth and twisted a blessing out of his dying father. Yet true blessing cannot be won through force or trickery. 'What is your name?' the stranger asks, and in doing so seizes the initiative. 'Jacob,' Jacob replies, 'Heel-catcher, Trickster' (for that is what the name seems to mean in these stories). Then, most mysteriously of all, the stranger gives him a new name and a new identity, and talks of 'striving with God' and 'prevailing'. Once before, God changed Abram's name to Abraham (Genesis 17:5). Is this 'man' *God*? Jacob himself begins to wonder. 'Tell me your name,' he says. The stranger refuses, as indeed God must, for God is and must remain a mystery, and *then* he blesses Jacob, and with the blessing the wrestling is over, and Jacob cries in amazement, 'I have seen God face to face!' while the sun, which set at Beth El (28:11) and has not been mentioned since, rises and floods him with its light.

Jacob has been wrestling with God! All is clear now. And he has a limp to prove it!

This story, so close to poetry, is one of the most profound in all scripture. No other story, outside the garden of Eden, puts God at such close quarters. No other story has God begging for mercy. No other story has God saying to another, 'You have prevailed.' The way this storyteller/poet has portrayed God is wonderfully daring. Such a vulnerable God is here, but one who cannot be defeated, one who releases himself from the grip of human beings by blessing them. Such a God reminds us of another, one who dies on a cross and yet remains triumphant, one who responds to human violence with blessing for all.

Yet there it is God who limps away, marked with the scars of crucifixion.

6 Unexpected forgiveness

Genesis 33:1–17

Having met with God, Jacob must meet his brother. He has wrestled with God all night, he has 'prevailed', he has been blessed, yet now he resorts to the plan of his earlier fear, dividing his entourage into two. And instead of running to greet his brother, he approaches him with his face to the ground, bowing seven times. He behaves like a rebellious vassal approaching an emperor who is ready to cut off his head. How different is this Jacob from the one Esau last encountered, the Jacob who made such a fool out of him over a bowl of lentil soup and a meal of game! He has never seen this Jacob before. How, then, does he respond? By running to meet him, embracing him, falling on his neck and kissing him! He does exactly what the father does in the parable of the prodigal son, when his son returns home!

Esau is amazed by the women and children Jacob has with him. But Jacob is bewildered also. He cannot take in his brother's forgiveness, for it is so far from what he expected. He looks into Esau's eyes and says, 'To see your face is like seeing the face of God!' He knows what he is talking about, for he has just seen God face to face. Then he offers Esau the blessing he stole from him. In verse 11 he uses a new word for 'present', not the same word in the Hebrew as the one for 'present' in verse 10. In verse 11 he uses the word for blessing. Esau receives it. The reconciliation is complete.

Or it would be, but for the promises of God. Jacob cannot return to Esau the promises he has received directly from God. He is destined for the land of Canaan; Esau is meant for Seir, as it is called here. Tragically, their ways must part, and Jacob is forced to make a feeble excuse to his brother about not being able to keep up with him.

Jacob and Esau are blood brothers kept apart by the purposes of God. That is how their story ends. These stories are wonderful, among the finest in all scripture, but still (in my opinion) they are flawed, spoiled by a God who chooses one and not another. The same God, limping away from Golgotha, will show us all another way.

Guidelines

God is both revealed and hidden in these stories of Jacob and Esau. In Genesis, the vision of God begins to get mixed up with national aspirations, and God becomes known as the God of Abraham, Isaac and Jacob, and not the God of Esau and Ishmael. We need to be honest about that, for still, all over the world, even where Christ is known and worshipped, the vision of God is spoiled by national aspirations.

Yet see how this storyteller portrays Esau! In chapter 27 he allows us to hear the pain of his rejection loud and clear, and in chapter 33 he makes him the hero of the piece, a man whose forgiveness and magnanimity are so startling that Jesus will find no better model for the character of the father in the parable of the prodigal son. That father shows us God, so Jacob is utterly right when he says to his brother in 33:10, 'To see your face is like seeing the face of God.' Except in the early story of the lentil soup, the storyteller refuses to criticize Esau. He presents him not as the enemy, but as the blood brother who shows us God. Wherever there are divisions and hatreds, as in Jacob's land today, Israel/Palestine, his stories need to be told again and heard.

> O God, our friend and unfailing companion,
> you who wrestle with us in the dark of our spoiled humanity,
> to answer our stranglehold with blessing,
> teach us to heed your word
> calling us to recognize one another as sisters and brothers
> and children of your love. Amen.

FURTHER READING

Michael Williams, (ed.), *The Storyteller's Companion to the Bible: Volume One: Genesis* (Abingdon Press, 1991)

Trevor Dennis, *Looking God in the Eye* (SPCK, 1998)

THE LETTERS OF JOHN

The apostle John was an energetic pastor and evangelist. He planted numerous churches across Asia Minor (modern-day western Turkey), with a ministry probably centred on the cosmopolitan city of Ephesus. John was one of the original Twelve chosen by Jesus, and as part of his witness to his Lord and Saviour he penned the fourth Gospel, written so that others 'may believe that Jesus is the Christ, the Son of God, and that by believing you may have life in his name' (John 20:31).

All was not well, however, in the churches for which John was pastorally responsible. They were being torn apart by severe disagreements about the gospel message. A group from the church began to claim special knowledge from God and the direct inspiration of the Holy Spirit, and yet taught things directly contrary to the apostolic message. They began to distort the truth about Jesus, suggesting that for the divine Christ to 'become flesh' was ridiculous and abhorrent. This wrong thinking led to wrong living: these prophets left the church, fought with it, and tried to drag others away to join their new sect.

Faced with this crisis, John writes to the Christian congregations to reassure them about the gospel message. He reminds them about the person and work of Jesus Christ, through whom we are 'born of God', are cleansed from our sins and receive eternal life. To a community which is theologically confused and prone to faction fighting, he emphasizes throughout his letters the twin themes of truth and love.

These notes use the English Standard Version (ESV).

1 Jesus—the word of life

1 John 1:1–4

As an apostle, John was an eye-witness to Jesus. He had been part of Jesus' intimate inner circle and spent three years travelling with him. He had listened to Jesus' teaching and been present at his transfiguration, crucifixion, resurrection appearances and ascension. So John launches into his letter with a declaration about Jesus Christ, the 'word of life'. Jesus is eternal—he was 'with the Father' from before time began, and has always existed 'from the beginning'. There are echoes here of the prologue to John's Gospel: 'In the beginning was the Word, and the Word was with God, and the Word was God' (John 1:1).

Yet, amazingly, the eternal Son of God was born in Bethlehem to the virgin Mary and grew up in first-century Palestine: he became a real human being, just like us. As John affirmed in his Gospel, 'the Word became flesh and dwelt among us, and we have seen his glory' (John 1:14). So here he testifies to the reality of the incarnation. John has personally seen Jesus Christ with his own eyes, heard him speak and physically touched him with his hands. The Christian message is about Jesus and is grounded on the historical events of his life, death and resurrection. It is not about an obscure theological system or make-believe, but about a real person who can be met and experienced. Are we actively looking to develop our relationship with Jesus? Or do we relegate him to the sidelines, even while we engage in numerous church activities?

John goes on to tell his readers that there are major implications in following Jesus. Through him we receive eternal life. Jesus is the word *of life*, the source and giver of life. It is to him that we must look for the richest and fullest life possible. Through Jesus we are brought into 'fellowship' with God (v. 3), no longer counted as his enemies but as his friends. Through him we also have fellowship with other Christians, an intimate sharing relationship. Because the false teachers troubling the church rejected the truth about Jesus, they missed out on both this life and this fellowship.

John is excited about the gospel message. The Christian good news is not something he can keep to himself, but he proclaims it openly. He writes to encourage and enthuse beleaguered Christians. Although their lives are difficult and their congregations struggling, they can take heart in this message of great joy (v. 4).

2 Sin and forgiveness

1 John 1:5—2:6

It is easy to grow complacent about our spiritual lives and think that we have 'made it', but the false teachers troubling the church in Asia Minor went even further. They claimed to be super-spiritual and to have reached such a state of religious perfection that sin was no longer an issue for them. They claimed to be intimate with God—to be truly 'enlightened', with a special knowledge of him. Yet they denied the truth about Jesus and their lives were characterized by major unrepented sin.

John explains that following God is not just about head-knowledge, but about an all-embracing way of life—or, to use a Jewish idiom, a way of walking. If we claim to be Christians, we must 'walk as Jesus walked' (2:6). Jesus is the only righteous human being ever to have lived. Since 'God is light', with a perfect and holy character, we must actively avoid the darkness and walk in the light. If we claim to follow him and yet happily dishonour him by our conduct, our profession of faith is a lie (1:6; 2:4). How seriously do we take our sin? Does it trouble us or do we dismiss it as trivial? When was the last time we stopped to examine the true state of our hearts before God? As we let the pure light of God shine upon us, we will come to a deeper realization of our need for forgiveness.

The wonderful message that John celebrates is that forgiveness is possible because of the death of Jesus on the cross. Christ's blood was shed so that all our sins might be washed away (1:7). As William Cowper writes in a famous hymn, 'There is a fountain filled with blood, drawn from Emmanuel's veins, and sinners plunged beneath that flood lose all their guilty stains.' Christ is a propitiation for our sins (2:2). In the Old Testament, innocent animals were sacrificed to turn away the righteous wrath of God from the guilty people. Now Christ himself, by his death on the cross, has become the ultimate sacrifice so that we can be rescued from divine punishment and restored to relationship with God.

This is very good news. It means that we can confess our sins to God in confidence that he will forgive us. God is faithful and just (1:9) and so takes into account the death of Jesus; and Jesus himself stands in the presence of God, as our advocate, presenting our case in the heavenly court. How awesome—the Son of God speaks up on our behalf.

3 Love one another

1 John 2:7–17

Apart from obeying God's commands and confessing our sins, what other evidence is there of whether we walk in the light or in the darkness? John explains that Christians will also love each other. This is one of his favourite themes, of particular significance to congregations who were suffering the results of bitter division.

In one sense, the command to love your neighbour as yourself was not new (v. 7). It had been around since the beginning of the Old Testament (Leviticus 19:18). But in another sense, this ancient command took on new form with the arrival of Jesus, and he himself called it 'new' (John 13:34). Jesus inaugurated a new era and was the first person ever to love others perfectly. Amazingly, John also expects this command to be fulfilled by us (v. 8).

Loving others is not the passport to fellowship with God, but it is evidence that we are already his disciples (vv. 9–11). Is this love evident in our lives? Do we work hard at relationships with other Christians? Do we love as Christ loves? It is easy to be deluded, going through the motions of church membership but still responding to others with indifference, bitterness, envy or even hatred. If we don't love others, we are blind and wandering around in the darkness.

We have a choice: either we can love God and his family, or we can love the world (vv. 15–17). There is no fence to sit on; we have to decide. By 'the world' John means not God's physical creation, but everything that is in opposition to God. This includes our sinful cravings and lusts, the attractive things that seduce us—like confidence in our status or material possessions. These worldly values can quickly invade the Church and corrupt us.

In the middle of this section, John writes a short symmetrical poem (vv. 12–14) to encourage his readers. 'Little children' is his favourite address for the whole congregation, but perhaps 'fathers' are mature believers and 'young men' recent converts. He reminds them of what they have already gained by following Jesus. They have been forgiven; they know the Father; they have overcome the evil one. These facts give us confidence when times are difficult.

4 Truth and error

1 John 2:18–27

So far, John has been pointing out the moral and ethical errors of those troubling the church: they hate God's people and they love sin. Now he shows also their serious doctrinal error. They deny one of the central tenets of the Christian faith, which is that the Son of God became a real human being—that Jesus (the man) is also the Christ (v. 22). John will have nothing to do with those who reject this truth: he calls them liars and antichrists. He does not try to find some 'middle ground', but makes a passionate and urgent appeal against these false prophets because they are leading others astray. They were once members of the church, but their departure is evidence that they were never truly Christians in the first place (v. 19). Such opposition to the gospel is what Jesus warned us to expect during the 'last days' or the 'last hour'—in other words, the last era of history between Jesus' ascension and his triumphant return.

Down the centuries there have always been false teachers pretending to be *bona fide* Christians. Many claim a special authority or prophetic endowment. How can we discern the difference between truth and error? How can we make sure we are not led astray by such impostors? John tells his readers that they have been given the gift of the Holy Spirit and are 'anointed by the Holy One'. They 'have knowledge' (v. 20). This anointing and this knowledge are given to all Christians, and teachers who claim secret insights or esoteric blessing should not be believed. Therefore Christians 'have no need that anyone should teach them' (v. 27). John is not questioning the validity of pastors who explain the Bible to their congregations, but he is challenging false prophets who claim access to extra divine knowledge.

In order to be secure in our faith, we must hold on to 'what we heard from the beginning' (v. 24)—to the historic facts of the gospel of Jesus Christ. Our society often denies the existence of objective truth, preferring 'experiential' truth, but the gospel is firmly rooted in history. The Holy Spirit affirms this historic faith and never teaches anything that diverges from it. This is the way, says John, that we are to judge whether spiritual anointing is real or counterfeit.

5 All will be revealed

1 John 2:28—3:10

John pauses in the middle of his letter to stand in wonder at what God has done for us: 'See what kind of love the Father has given to us, that we should be called children of God' (3:1). This is staggering—arrogant rebels against God now adopted as his children, 'born of him' (2:29). We don't deserve God's overflowing love, but he takes the initiative to welcome us into his family. For Christians, that change of status has already taken place: we are God's children *now*. And there are more amazing things in store for us when Christ returns. As the apostle Paul writes, 'No eye has seen, nor ear heard, nor the heart of man imagined, what God has prepared for those who love him' (1 Corinthians 2:9). This tremendous gospel reality is a great encouragement even when the world is giving us a hard time.

The imminent return of Christ is a fresh impetus for faithfulness. On that great day, there will be two possible reactions: either we will be confident before him or we will be ashamed and shrink away (2:28). His second advent will reveal the truth of our relationships: either we are children of God or we are 'of the devil'. Pretence will no longer be possible. Sin is nothing less than rebellion against God and breaking his holy law (3:4), but if we are born of God, we will reflect his righteous character, just as a child bears the family likeness. The evidence of our spiritual rebirth is not some ecstatic experience, but a changed life. If we know God, then we will imitate God.

Often we put up with sin too easily. When was the last time we stopped to consider the ways in which our attitudes and actions offend God? Are we really bothered by our sin or have we grown blasé?

John again makes a strong case for the imperative of holiness. He does not think we can be perfect (he has already said the opposite in 1:8–10), but most of us by now should have made more progress towards holiness than we have done. Yet, thanks be to God, the sinless Jesus Christ has come into the world to take away our sins (3:5) and to destroy the devil's work (3:8).

6 Love in action

1 John 3:11–24

What a contrast there is between the spiritual position of Christian believers and the position of unbelievers! Often it seems hard to tell the difference, but the reality is stark. As John explains, the first group possess life—eternal life, which we already enjoy. The second are living in death. The first love one another; the second are motivated by 'hate'.

Two examples show us these differences. Cain is a warning to us (vv. 12–15). He was in league with the devil and murdered (literally 'butchered') his righteous brother, Abel (see Genesis 4). Those who are opposed to the Christian gospel are spurred on, says John, by the same sort of hate, whether they realize it or not. We abhor murder and yet tend quickly to justify ourselves when we get angry with others. But in his Sermon on the Mount, Jesus connects these two sins and says that they both spring from a hateful heart (Matthew 5:21–22).

In contrast to Cain, Jesus Christ provides a positive example that we should emulate (vv. 16–18). His love for others was so great that he laid down his life for us. Although he possessed more than we can possibly imagine, he was prepared to give it up for us (Philippians 2:5–11). Does our love for others demonstrate the same quality of self-sacrifice? Mere rhetoric about love is no good without visible action, such as giving our material possessions to those in need. We must love not just 'in word or talk' but 'in deed and in truth'.

Of course, the death of Jesus is much more than just an ethical model—it is not simply a touching demonstration of the love of God. The cross of Christ also achieves something. It opens the way to relationship with God, because Jesus died *for us*—on our behalf, in our place. As the prophet Isaiah declares, 'He was wounded for *our* transgressions, *he* was crushed for *our* iniquities; upon *him* was the chastisement that brought *us* peace, and with *his* stripes *we* are healed' (Isaiah 53:5). Therefore we can be confident of our relationship with God, because it depends not on how we feel about him but on what he has done for us through Jesus. Sometimes we feel insecure about our salvation, but even if our hearts (or our consciences) condemn us, God overrides the verdict (v. 20). When we grasp this great truth, we will find fresh boldness in God's presence, especially in prayer (vv. 21–22).

Guidelines

'By this we know love, that he laid down his life for us' (1 John 3:16).

Here is love vast as the ocean,
Loving kindness as the flood,
When the Prince of Life, our Ransom,
Shed for us his precious blood.
Who his love will not remember?
Who can cease to sing his praise?
He can never be forgotten
Throughout heaven's eternal days.

On the mount of crucifixion
Fountains opened deep and wide;
Through the floodgates of God's mercy
Flowed a vast and gracious tide.
Grace and love, like mighty rivers,
Poured incessant from above,
And heaven's peace and perfect justice
Kissed a guilty world in love.
WILLIAM REES (1802–83), TRANSLATED BY WILLIAM EDWARDS (1848–1929)

Take time to pause and wonder at the extent of God's love for us displayed in Jesus Christ. Like the apostle John and his readers, we have much for which to praise God. For instance:

- God's initiative in rescuing us
- God's breaking into the world in the person of his Son
- the death of Jesus, that our sins might be forgiven
- eternal life and fellowship with God that comes through Jesus
- the confidence we can have in God's presence
- our brothers and sisters in Christ

1 Test what you hear

1 John 4:1–6

Numerous religious movements and philosophies compete for our attention, many claiming to represent some new truth or spiritual insight. In a society where tolerance is the pre-eminent virtue, it can often be difficult to declare someone else's views wrong and unacceptable, but John warns that we must be ready to test every religious idea and to distance ourselves from those which are dangerous or misleading.

There are two spirits active in the world—the Spirit of truth and the spirit of error. Many fraudulent prophets claim to be spiritually enlightened, yet actually speak by 'the spirit of antichrist'. John offers us two tests of their validity.

The first test is what the teachers say about Jesus (vv. 2–3). The Holy Spirit always glorifies Jesus Christ. He affirms the gospel truth that the man Jesus of Nazareth is also the divine Word of God, both fully human and fully divine. As we have seen, this was an issue particularly troubling the church in John's day. In our day, it may be other gospel essentials which are challenged and need to be re-affirmed—such as the divinity of Jesus, his physical resurrection or the reality of his return. John urgently warns us that the spirit of antichrist, who is in league with the devil, wants to lead people away from Jesus. Thankfully, the power of this spirit pales into complete insignificance compared with the tremendous power of the Holy Spirit (v. 4), and so we do not need to fear.

The second test is who listens to the teachers (vv. 5–6). Where do their philosophies find a following? It is no surprise to find that false prophets are accepted by the world, whereas those who have fellowship with God listen to the Spirit of God and are able to discern the truth. If some new teaching is rejected by the wider Church and yet accepted by the world, we must be on guard—it may have originated with the spirit of error.

Are we prepared to take our stand for the truths of historic Christianity? Do we respond with serious thought to new challenges to the gospel today? Do we take time to read the scriptures and listen to the Spirit of God? John calls us to be actively testing what we hear.

2 God is love

1 John 4:7–21

John returns to one of his favourite themes—love. He makes the profound statement that 'God is love' (v. 8). It is not just that love comes from God (v. 7) or that God loves (v. 11), but God *is* love. Love is the very essence of his being. As John proclaims in his Gospel, 'God so loved the world that he gave his only Son, that whoever believes in him should not perish but have eternal life' (John 3:16). We did not love God first, but he took the initiative to love us and send us Jesus, even when we were rebels against him. Once again, John celebrates the fact that Jesus is a propitiation for our sins: on the cross he turned away the wrath of God, paying the penalty we owed. Jesus died that we might live for ever (v. 9). Now he has also given us the gift of his Holy Spirit (v. 13), who brings new spiritual life and equips us for Christian service.

Jesus often linked the dual commands to love God and love our neighbour (for example, Matthew 22:34–40), and here John does the same. God's love is shown in Jesus, and if we claim to love God then we must love other people as he loves them. It is not that loving others brings us into fellowship with God, but our fellowship with God is shown by our love for others. If we have genuinely met with God, then the way we behave should be radically transformed. This is a vital piece of evidence that we are Christians. If our relationships are still characterized by bitterness, envy, harsh words or manipulation, then we are lying when we say we follow Jesus (vv. 7–8, 19–21). John explains that whoever does not love cannot possibly know God. He leads here by example. He is a pastor who dearly loves his congregations and often addresses them as 'beloved'.

What is our motivation to love others? Is it fear of the wrath of God or experience of the love of God? Perfect love casts out fear (v. 18) and therefore, as his followers, we can have confidence before God on the day of judgment. We are not issued with threats to obey God, but his love compels us to imitate him. His initiative to love us should inspire us to a life of whole-hearted devotion to God and of self-sacrificial service to our fellow Christians.

3 Being born of God

1 John 5:1–12

Those who believe in Jesus Christ, who submit to him as their Saviour and Lord, have been 'born of God'. This radical spiritual transformation is what Jesus calls being 'born again' by the Spirit (see John 3). New birth brings a new beginning: our old way of life is left behind and we start afresh with an entirely different perspective. We love God and also begin to love our fellow Christians (vv. 1–2).

Those who are born again obey God's commands. However, his law is not 'burdensome', not an irksome list of rules and regulations. As Jesus explained, his yoke is easy and his burden is light (Matthew 11:30). Obeying God's commands brings spiritual freedom and true life in all its fullness, and, because of our faith in Jesus, he gives us the resources to overcome the sinful tendencies of the world (vv. 3–5). How are we doing in that daily battle against sin? Do we experience 'victory' as we obey God's commands?

Yet we need assurance, when the battle is at its hottest, that we have made the right decision in following Jesus. How can we be certain that our salvation comes through him, and that this is not just wishful thinking? John explains that the testimony about Jesus is confirmed by three witnesses—the water, the blood and the Spirit (vv.

6–9). The first two probably refer to Jesus' incarnational ministry, from his baptism in the River Jordan (water) to his crucifixion at Golgotha (blood). Some false teachers thought that the heavenly 'Christ' descended on the man 'Jesus' at his baptism and then soon departed. But again John affirms the reality of the incarnation: the man Jesus Christ, the Son of God, lived a real life and died a real death on a real cross. The Holy Spirit testifies about Jesus and will never say anything that contradicts these central gospel facts. These truths are what we need to cling on to and be assured by when life is tough. It is a message confirmed by God himself (v. 9).

Following Jesus, being 'born again', experiencing the victory of faith, is not just a personal preference or some theoretical debate. It is about nothing less than eternal life and eternal death. Without Jesus, says John, we do not have life—we are spiritually dead. But with Jesus, we have the richest possible life—eternal life that begins now. Are we living as people who have been born again by the Spirit, with radically changed lives?

4 Be confident

1 John 5:13–21

John is writing to a church which is in the midst of turmoil. The Christians are probably confused and depressed and wondering whether it is worth carrying on. So their pastor ends his letter by boosting their confidence. He wants them to have assurance—to know for certain the truth of their convictions. Many people today claim that we cannot be certain about anything, but John strongly disagrees. Again and again he repeats the declaration, 'We know… we know… we know'.

We know that through Jesus Christ we have eternal life (v. 13). Our confidence is shown in our boldness before God. We do not hang back, but approach him with the privilege of children, in the certain knowledge that he hears us and will answer. John instructs us to pray according to God's will—listening to his voice and following the leading of his Spirit (vv. 14–15). It is easy to pray for things that we imagine will benefit us, without pausing to consider whether they are possibly God's will. John does not explain why God sometimes answers our petitions with 'no' or 'wait' instead of 'yes', but our role is to ask boldly and persistently, trusting God for the result.

John ends with another appeal that we keep ourselves from sin. Although we have been 'born of God', we still live in a world that lies in the grip of the 'evil one' (vv. 18–19). Opportunities to sin abound, but our goal as Christians should be to become each day more like Jesus, the one holy, perfect person. Do we take sin in our lives seriously or are we so used to it that we fail to notice it any more? If we see other Christians sinning, our immediate response, rather than gossiping about them or gleefully condemning them, should be to pray for them to be restored. That is, unless their sin 'leads to death'. Probably John has in mind those false teachers who are troubling the church, who arrogantly reject God. They have tasted salvation but have thrown it back in God's face, and thus miss out on eternal life through Jesus.

John's last words are not a conventional greeting or blessing, but an exhortation to 'keep ourselves from idols' (v. 21). Anything that competes in our affections with God is idolatrous. We are in trouble if our driving desire in life is to gain influence, accumulate wealth or please our families, instead of to glorify God. We must pull down any idols and ensure that God alone remains in first place.

5 John's second letter

2 John

John writes to a local congregation ('the elect lady', v. 1), perhaps meeting in someone's house, to remind them of some of the things he has said in his longer letter. Once again, his twin themes are truth and love. He celebrates their faithfulness and obedience to God's commandments, as well as their love for one another (vv. 1–6).

Because John loves this congregation, however, he also wants to warn them about a dangerous deception being practised. There have been numerous defections from the church by those who reject a central tenet of the gospel (the incarnation of Christ) and, as in his earlier letter, John rebukes these seceders harshly as deceivers and antichrists (v. 7). They think they are spiritually superior to normal

Christians and that they have grown out of their early faith, but actually they no longer 'abide' in the teaching of Christ. Therefore it is as if they have rejected God himself (v. 9).

To the beleaguered Christians who remain, John gives two specific instructions. First, they must 'watch themselves' (v. 8). We must be careful not to wander off track but to stick to the teaching of Christ, so that we receive our full reward. Are we aiming to win this glorious eternal reward from God, or are we motivated by the tarnished and temporary prizes the world has to offer?

Second, John instructs the Christians not to receive false prophets into their house (vv. 10–11). This seems surprising, because the New Testament usually encourages generous hospitality, especially to strangers (Romans 12:13; 1 Peter 4:9–10). John does not mean that we should refuse to show friendship to non-Christians, but that we should not give official welcome to falsehood in our congregations (which, in John's day, met in someone's house). He knows that the local church will not survive if serious error is tolerated or even sanctioned in its midst. Christians who welcome these deceivers in effect contribute to their 'wicked works' (v. 11). In contrast, as a true teacher, John is confident that he will be received with joy when they meet (v. 12).

6 John's third letter

3 John is the shortest letter in the New Testament (just 219 words in Greek). It is a brief note, dashed off in a hurry, and without the doctrinal content of John's first two letters. It is the only book in the New Testament not to mention Jesus or Christ, although John does refer to 'the name' (v. 7).

The reason for John's note is a crisis in a local house church, led by Diotrephes. Diotrephes was dividing the congregation. He had rejected John's pastoral oversight and was spreading malicious rumours about him. Perhaps Diotrephes was a false teacher, but more probably he was just a power-hungry individual. The language John uses of him is mild when compared to his fiery polemic against the heretics in 1 John and 2 John. John has tried persistently to bring Diotrephes back into the fold. First he had written, but his letter was disregarded. Next he had sent missionaries to visit, but they too were rejected. Diotrephes even threatened to throw out of the church anyone who sided with John (vv. 9–10). So now John plans to visit personally and confront his opponent face to face.

The delegation sent by John had, however, been received warmly by Gaius (v. 5)—perhaps the leader of another local house church. The apostle therefore writes to Gaius, commending his hospitality and encouraging him to continue in it. He praises Gaius as a faithful brother who 'walks in the truth' and loves the church (vv. 1–8), instructing him to 'imitate good' (v. 11). This private letter is sent with Demetrius as courier (v. 12).

Which of these two protagonists are we most like? Do we sometimes display the arrogance and pride of Diotrephes and tend to be autocratic in our conduct, to gossip against those with whom we disagree and encourage divisions in the Christian community? Or are we more like Gaius, a humble servant, showing love and warm hospitality? It is Gaius who is commended.

Guidelines

'God is love… perfect love casts out fear' (1 John 4:16, 18).

Love bade me welcome, yet my soul drew back,
    Guilty of dust and sin.
But quick-eyed Love, observing me grow slack
    From my first entrance in,
Drew nearer to me, sweetly questioning
    If I lacked anything.
'A guest', I answered, 'worthy to be here':
    Love said, 'You shall be he.'
'I, the unkind, ungrateful? Ah, my dear,
    I cannot look on Thee.'
Love took my hand, and smiling did reply,
    'Who made the eyes but I?'
'Truth, Lord; but I have marred them; let my shame
    Go where it doth deserve.'

'And know you not', says Love, *'who bore the blame?'*
    'My dear, then I will serve.'
'You must sit down', says Love, *'and taste my meat.'*
    So I did sit and eat.
GEORGE HERBERT (1593–1633)

John encourages us to be confident in God's presence and to pray boldly. Therefore take time to pray for some of the concerns that the apostle has raised in his letters. For example:
* that we would better imitate Christ
* that we would be concerned about our sin and that of our society
* that we would grow in our love for God and for each other
* that we would hold on to the truth about Jesus as taught by the apostles
* that we would listen closely to the Holy Spirit

FURTHER READING

Dianne Tidball, *John's Letters* (Crossway Bible Guide, 2002)—an accessible introduction, useful devotionally

David Jackman, *The Message of John's Letters* (Bible Speaks Today series, 1988)—clear expositions from a well-known Bible teacher

Gary M. Burge, *The Letters of John* (NIV Application Commentary, 1996)—serious about both the meaning of the text and its application in the 21st century

Colin G. Kruse, *The Letters of John* (Pillar New Testament Commentary, 2000)—detailed scholarship with pastoral sensitivity

THROUGH PARADOX TO TRANSFORMATION

The New Testament is shot through with paradox, a notion described by the psychoanalyst Carl Jung as the 'synthesis of opposites'. Paradox catches our attention because it goes against the grain and defies expectation. It is uncomfortable, and it can be profoundly threatening. This gives it great power as an agent of psychological and spiritual change.

Paradox signifies tension and conflict. Psychologists have long recognized that the resolution of inner psychological conflict can be the occasion for the development of healthy beliefs, behaviour patterns and personal relationships. Unfortunately, people may also deal with conflict in a way that is unhelpful or unhealthy. This can clearly be seen in the Gospel accounts, which tell of the diverse responses of people to the paradox presented to them in the person of Jesus.

The threat posed by paradox can be dealt with by simply rejecting it as nonsense or contradiction, so that existing beliefs and assumptions about the way the world is remain intact. Alternatively, it can lead to a reappraisal of those beliefs and assumptions, allowing them to develop and grow or, more radically, to be turned upside down. *Paradox can result in transformation*.

Over the next two weeks we will consider some examples of the way in which the New Testament uses the paradox of Jesus Christ as a starting point in the transformation of the believer. We will begin with Jesus' own teaching, by word and action, then move on to reflect on the resurrection and its effect on the disciples. Finally we will consider the meaning of transformation in our own Christian lives. These notes use the New Revised Standard Version (NRSV).

1 Growing seeds: a picture from nature

Mark 4:26–32

The first of these two parables is unique to Mark's Gospel; the second is also found in Matthew (13:31–32) and Luke (13:18–19), with a version in the Gospel of Thomas (Gospel of Thomas, 20). A reference to grain falling into the earth is also found in John's Gospel (see below). From this we can conclude that the image of a growing seed was well established in the earliest oral traditions of the sayings of Jesus. The significance he attached to it is at the heart of his teaching.

The image of the growing seed must have been highly meaningful to both Jesus and his audience in rural Galilee. It is easy to imagine him watching the process of sowing and harvest from his earliest years, and reflecting on its deeper significance. Jesus uses this familiar event from the natural world to make otherwise difficult paradoxes digestible. In using the natural world so readily in his teaching, Jesus is acknowledging that the created order, if seen in the right way, can tell us something about its maker.

Jesus is talking about the kingdom of God—that is, the way that things are when God is in charge in people's lives. The simile of the mustard seed (vv. 30–32) tells us that the apparently small, useless and trivial can be phenomenally big, useful and significant. This happens through a process of transformation that is hidden and mysterious (v. 27).

Jesus is clear that the tiny seed and the great shrub are both mustard—the plant's essential identity is retained even in the face of such dramatic change. The seed isn't dug up and replaced with an imported shrub by the BBC *Ground Force* team. The seed *becomes* the shrub.

This image is developed further in John 12, where Jesus applies it both to his own death and resurrection, and also to Christian discipleship: 'Very truly, I tell you, unless a grain of wheat falls into the earth and dies, it remains just a single grain; but if it dies, it bears much fruit' (John 12:24). The grain is not only little and becomes big;

through death, it becomes alive. Jesus' central message is that God can take our small minds and cold hearts and, in a way that is hidden and mysterious—but in some sense involves our dying—he can transform us.

2 The beatitudes

Matthew 5:3–12

Matthew's version of the beatitudes, the cornerstone of the Sermon on the Mount, is a beautifully constructed piece of rhythmical Greek poetry that could easily be learnt by heart. These verses may have been used in the basic instruction of new Christians, or in formal worship in the earliest churches. They were at the heart of the Christian message from the very beginning, and are of the greatest importance.

The original poem ends at verse 10, and this makes it clear that the meat of the poem is sandwiched between two statements about the kingdom of heaven (Matthew's idiom for the kingdom of God). So again, we have a description of the way things are when God is in charge in people's lives.

But what do the beatitudes mean? We have grown so used to hearing them that it is easy to ignore the astonishing nature of their message. The first half of verses 3, 4, 5, 6, 10 and 11 appear to be frank contradictions. This comes across more clearly if we remember that the Greek word usually translated 'blessed' can also mean 'happy'. 'Happy are those who mourn' sounds uncomfortably like insensitive nonsense.

This use of extreme paradox is indeed intended to bring the listener up short, to raise questions, to challenge assumptions. It is also the starting point for a description of God's transforming action. In each of these verses a paradox is presented, and is immediately explained by a description of a transformed situation when God is in charge. God's transforming action is crucially described as something that happens both now (v. 3) and in the future. Jesus' descriptions of God's kingdom as something that is in a continuous process of 'becoming' (see, for instance, Mark 1:15) mirror our experience of living the Christian journey.

In the beatitudes, we are presented with a message that is about as far from a 'health and wealth' gospel as it is possible to get. Instead there is a promotion of poverty, humility, mercy, reconciliation, seeking after God, and an embracing of suffering. This a radical reaffirmation of God's covenant with his people, firmly rooted in the Old Testament prophetic tradition: 'He has told you, O mortal, what is good; and what does the Lord require of you but to do justice, and to love kindness, and to walk humbly with your God?' (Micah 6:8).

3 Jesus the servant

John 13:3–17

As we noted yesterday, humility is a key component, if not *the* key component, of the message of Jesus. It is a notion that clearly caused the leaders among his disciples some difficulty, at both the intellectual and the emotional level. Jesus did not just use words to drive home his paradoxical message about humility. On one occasion he used a child as a visual image (Matthew 18:1–4). In our culture, where children are increasingly being pressurized to 'grow up' and behave like adults, Jesus' profound respect for childhood still appears radical.

Jesus' actions during the last supper as described by John are perhaps even more shocking. They certainly shocked Peter. Yet, if his teaching up until that time had been properly understood, this is precisely the sort of thing one might have expected Jesus to do (see, for instance, Mark 10:43). Perhaps Peter had misunderstood Jesus' teaching, or perhaps he had thought that although Jesus could 'talk the talk', he would never actually 'walk the walk'. In fact, through acting out his teaching about humility, Jesus at once clarified it and invested it with personal authority. He demonstrated the integrity of spiritual truth and physical action that is so characteristic of his ministry and, at a deeper level, of the incarnation itself.

This action of Jesus is a very rich source of theological understanding in many ways, but at its most basic it tells us something about the nature of Christian leadership. To be a leader is to be a servant, literally and metaphorically. There is no place for the trappings of power or wealth among Christian leaders. Christian leaders are called constantly to wrestle with the issue of how to express their servanthood in actions as well as words.

Christians who are in positions of power in their workplace or local community are also called to live out this message. To be able to demonstrate that leadership can really mean loving service, rather than self-advancement, is a key way that we can bear witness to the gospel in our world.

4 A reflection on the servanthood of Jesus

Philippians 2:5–11

Jesus' actions not only illustrate his teaching; they are also an example for the believer to follow. In this passage from the letter to the Philippians, Paul uses the humility of Jesus as a model for the behaviour of the Christian.

Many scholars believe that, perhaps like Matthew's beatitudes, these verses (6–11) are an early Christian hymn, naturally falling into three or six stanzas. If this is so, Paul is using material that is well known to his audience and applying it to a specific aspect of their situation, very much as a modern preacher or pastor might do. If this material does represent something that was very early and very well known, it can tell us a lot about the central concerns of the first Christians as they reflected on the life and death of Jesus.

First, they saw in the life of Jesus a perfect model of humility and obedience to God. They had no doubt that Jesus had really lived and really died, and that the manner of his death had been shockingly humiliating. The comment 'even death on a cross' (v. 8) is thought by some to be an insertion by Paul himself, an expression of his revulsion, as a strict Jew, at the idea of crucifixion. (We will consider Paul's feelings about the cross in more detail next week.) Immediately after this comment comes an amazing 'Therefore' (v. 9), a paradox that forms the central pivot of these verses. Because of, not in spite of, the miserable and sordid circumstances of Jesus' obedient death, God has exalted him. The language that is used to describe this exaltation tells us that the earliest Christians had rapidly come to an understanding of the divine nature of Jesus Christ (verse 10 is a direct quotation of

Isaiah 45:23, a passage referring unambiguously to God) and they had reached this understanding in the light of the resurrection. Somehow, in a way hidden and mysterious, yet purposeful, God had transformed the worst of situations into the best of situations.

Philippians is a letter that is full of joy. The complete turning of ideas on their heads, expressed so powerfully in these verses, at first startles but then liberates. No situation is so desperate that it cannot be turned inside out and back to front by God's action if we, having the mind of Christ Jesus, are obedient to his voice.

5 The resurrection, part one: the empty tomb

Mark 16:1–8

As we noted yesterday, it was the experience of the resurrection that enabled the followers of Jesus to gain a full understanding of the nature of his mission and identity, in a way that had just not been possible before. The resurrection is an underwriting of Jesus' teaching about the paradoxical and transforming nature of the kingdom of God, because it demonstrates God's definitive transforming action in Jesus' own person.

But, just as with the seed in the ground, the process of the resurrection remains hidden and mysterious. Nobody saw Jesus rise from the dead. The women who were intent on caring for the dead body of Jesus were instead confronted with an empty tomb and an angel, signifying the presence of God. Mark's vivid description of their experience is wholly psychologically authentic.

When we are confronted with ideas that threaten our assumptions about the way the world is, we become surprised, uncomfortable and anxious. When we are confronted by events that are so entirely novel that we can make no sense of them, that are beyond our experience or expectation, we are terrified. This can be readily observed in babies and small children, for whom much of the world is novel. You may have experienced something of this emotion on 11 September 2001.

The cognitive response of amazement and the emotional response of terror went hand in hand for these women (v. 8). But, as Jesus himself had so often done, the angel addressed their anxiety, telling them not to be afraid and reassuring them that things really were all right. This seems to have had little effect on them, at least at first.

The women were caught up in one part of a process that would be understood only with hindsight. It is as if they had tasted the first half of the Philippians 'hymn' or the beatitude verses without yet having the benefit of the whole story. There was pain and tension, but not yet resolution. The emotional trauma experienced by these women is a measure of the momentous nature of the event that was taking place. One reason that the resurrection had such a transforming effect on the psychology of the first Christians, on both their beliefs and actions, is the massive emotional response that it evoked. Meditating on the feelings of these women may be one way for us to begin to experience that transformation for ourselves.

6 The resurrection, part two: a transformed Jesus
Luke 24:13–35

The concept of 'journey' is very important in Luke's Gospel. This story tells of a journey that ends in transformation. Crucially, the transformation is achieved through a meeting with Jesus.

The two disciples who embarked on the journey knew all about the empty tomb and the message of the angels, but this was not sufficient to convince them that Jesus had risen from the dead. Like the women, they were amazed (v. 22), and were effectively fleeing the scene of the action. Rather than abject terror, however, their emotions were dominated by bitter disappointment, doubt and perplexity.

Jesus began by drawing alongside them and drawing out from them their thoughts and their feelings. He then dealt with their confusion of mind by a careful explanation, setting the recent apparently meaningless events in the context of the existing worldview of the disciples. That is, he applied familiar scriptural texts to his own death and resurrection. The grounding of his argument in the scriptures provided security, but the way that scripture was radically reinterpreted and applied to these events was tremendously challenging. Thus Jesus set the scene for a dramatic transformation of intellectual categories in his listeners. This, indeed, seems to have taken place. The exhilaration that can accompany this sort of cognitive shift is described in verse 32: 'Were not our hearts burning within us while he was talking to us on the road, while he was opening the scriptures to us?'

But these disciples were left with a lot more than the sense that the resurrection is a great and glorious theological idea. They came to believe that it had actually happened, and that Jesus was alive. They believed because, in the end, they recognized that they were in his living presence. As in most accounts of the resurrection appearances, Jesus was not at first recognized by the disciples. The risen Jesus seems to have been like a completely different person. And yet, in just the way that he had described the transformation of the seed to the plant, he remained essentially the same.

This 'essential Jesus' was recognized on the basis of simple words or gestures that had an intimate significance to his followers, that were associated with precious memories or deep needs (John 20:16, 27; 21:6–7; Acts 9:5). It was this sense of a love enduring beyond death that led them to proclaim, 'The Lord has risen indeed!' (v. 34).

Guidelines

Our own transformation begins with seeing Jesus in perhaps un-expected people, places and situations. This prayer is for openness to the experience of God's presence at such times:

O gracious and holy Father,
give us wisdom to perceive you,
intelligence to understand you,
diligence to seek you, patience to wait for you,
eyes to behold you, and a life to proclaim you,
through the power of the Spirit
of our Lord Jesus Christ.
St Benedict

1 Christian transformation: being born again

John 3:1–8

This week, we will reflect on the transformation that occurs in the life of the Christian. This transformation is reflected in changes in beliefs and behaviour, but, as Jesus makes clear in this conversation with Nicodemus, it is fundamentally a spiritual process. As with the growing seed, and as with Jesus' own resurrection, the work of the Spirit is invisible, seen only through the outcome of its actions. This is why the metaphor of wind is so apt.

This is the one place in John's Gospel where 'kingdom of God' language occurs, and it is important to note just how similar this teaching is to that found in the Synoptic Gospels. Jesus is saying that where God is in charge in the life of a person, there is a complete transformation, a rejection of the values of the flesh in favour of spiritual values. So radical is this transformation that it is like being born again as a new person.

The term 'flesh', in this context, does not refer to the physical body but rather to the values of the world, values that are so masterfully undercut by the beatitudes. So, for a person to become a Christian and grow as a Christian does not mean neglecting the body; it means a lifelong embracing of the values of the kingdom of God.

Paul takes up this theme in 2 Corinthians, likening the transformation of the believer to the transformation of Jesus in the resurrection: 'From now on, therefore, we regard no one from a human point of view*; even though we once knew Christ from a human point of view*, we know him no longer in that way. So if anyone is in Christ, there is a new creation: everything old has passed away; see, everything has become new!' (2 Corinthians 5:16–17; *literally 'according to the flesh').

The transformation of Jesus is a model for and a guarantee of our own transformation. Making a decision to follow Jesus Christ and being baptized are highly significant first, not last, steps in this process. This is made clear in the original Greek of the 2 Corinthians passage. The tense of 'become' in verse 17 indicates something that has started and is continuing. Just like the kingdom of God, we are in a process of 'becoming'. Jesus taught us how to claim this as a reality when we pray, 'Your kingdom come.'

2 The transformation of the first disciples

Acts 4:8–20

The Gospels tell us that the Roman administration in Jerusalem colluded with the temple theocracy to bring about the death of Jesus. Jesus was executed under Roman law by a method that was routinely applied to insurrectionists who posed a threat to Roman rule. But Pontius Pilate, a man not otherwise known for his restraint in such matters (Luke 13:1), extraordinarily did not see fit to round up and dispose of the key members of Jesus' movement. This tells us that the perceived threat was from Jesus himself. His followers were treated as insignificant, and are indeed described in pathetic terms in the Gospel accounts.

Political and religious resistance movements were quite common at this time, and their leaders sometimes claimed to be the Messiah. When a leader died, this did not necessarily spell the end of the movement, which might regroup under a male relative of its original leader.

Nothing like this happened to the Jesus movement. James the brother of Jesus did not seize power and begin to carry out 'Jesus policies' with the help of the other disciples. The memory of Jesus was not revered or 'kept alive' by a band of disciples who had managed to pull themselves together after the trauma of the crucifixion and the grief of bereavement. Instead, there emerged a deep conviction among the disciples that Jesus had been raised. They were transformed from people who wanted only to hide and keep silent to people who could not help shouting their message from the rooftops (v. 20).

Just as in the passage we looked at yesterday, Luke makes it very clear that this change, beginning with an encounter with the risen Jesus, has been effected through the continuing action of the Holy Spirit (v. 8). The Spirit enabled Peter and John to do things that seemed beyond their human capabilities (v. 13) but, more than this, the Spirit made them Christ-like.

Peter was a man whose courage had finally failed him in the court-yard of the house of the high priest. Now, when he is brought before the high priestly family, he is recognized as a follower of Jesus not because of his northern accent but because of his courage and elo-quence (v. 13). In this, as in their compassionate approach to the lame man (v. 9), Peter and John have come to resemble Jesus.

3 The transformation of Paul

Acts 9:1–9

Luke tells us that Paul met Jesus on the road to Damascus. Paul himself speaks of this encounter in 1 Corinthians 15 and Galatians 1. Paul talks of being 'untimely born' (1 Corinthians 15:8). This is prob-ably a reference to the fact that he had not known Jesus during his earthly life, but it also describes the traumatic nature of his conversion (or rebirth). There is no doubt that Paul's meeting with Jesus caused him great distress of mind, signified by blindness in Luke's account.

The disciples on the road to Emmaus had an existing relationship of trust and hope in Jesus. This enabled them gradually to understand and accept what Jesus was telling them on the way. In contrast, when Paul met Jesus his whole *raison d'être* was shattered. He was con-fronted with overwhelming conflict or, in Jung's terms, with opposites that could not be synthesized. The conflict was between his experi-ence of Jesus and his most deeply held beliefs. When there is extreme conflict between experience and beliefs, something has to give, and indeed Paul appears to have become a broken man for a time.

Paul had not known Jesus before, so he could not 'recognize' him. However, he instinctively fell to his feet and addressed him as 'Lord' (v. 5). Paul was worshipping Jesus, but Jesus, significantly identifying himself with the words '*I am...*', instead described Paul as his persecutor. Why was Paul so zealous in his persecution of the first Christians? One reason seems to have been the offensive nature of their message. They preached a *crucified* and risen Messiah. For someone who, by his own admission, was scrupulously devoted to the

Torah, this was not just an interesting intellectual paradox—it was a disgusting perversion of Judaism. In his letter to the Galatians, Paul reflects on the statement in Deuteronomy 21:23, 'Cursed is everyone who hangs on a tree', but then immediately talks about his own experience of Jesus in precisely the opposite terms, as the mediator of God's blessing (Galatians 3:13–14).

Just like the other disciples, Paul's experience of the risen Jesus was characterized by love, a sense of being intimately known, called by name, and 'taken hold of' (Philippians 3:12, NIV). This is what, in the end, turned the cross on its head, from a painful stumbling-block into the joyous core of his gospel (1 Corinthians 1:23). This is what transformed Paul.

4 The renewing of the mind

Romans 11:33—12:2

Sometimes the letters of Paul are talked about as if they were the dreariest of theology textbooks. But it would be a strange textbook indeed in which the author now and again broke into song to praise God, the subject of his text, or disclosed his most intimate moments in the presence of God. One of the delights of reading Paul is that he does this repeatedly. At some times, logical argument fails him as a vehicle to contain the mysteries of which he is speaking; at others, he just cannot help but speak of the joy he has found in his relationship with Christ Jesus.

This doxology comes at the end of a very difficult portion in the letter to the Romans in which Paul seems to be reaching the limits of what can be explained or understood by human intellect. It is a free acknowledgment of the gulf between human knowledge and the mind of God, of the presumption inherent in human attempts to understand God.

But Paul does not give up and say that therefore it is impossible to know God. Instead, he urges his readers to allow their minds to be renewed, no longer conformed to human values and thought patterns, but tuned in to the will of God. Part of the new creation that begins when a person becomes a Christian is a change of mind, which goes hand-in-hand with holiness of life. The Christian mind is primarily a vehicle for discernment with a view to obedience. Having this 'mind of Christ' (1 Corinthians 2:16; Philippians 2:5) means being open to the paradoxical nature of Jesus' life and teaching, his death and resurrection, and applying it to one's own situation. This underpins spiritual transformation.

At the beginning of this week, we noted that Jesus himself gave us the means for starting on a journey of transformation in the words, 'Your kingdom come.' Today's passage draws to our attention the fact that the coming of God's kingdom begins with obedience to his will in the life of the believer: 'Your will be done, on earth as it is in heaven.'

5 The transformed life

Romans 12:3–21

Continuing from where we left off yesterday, Paul unpacks what he means by a life that is acceptable to God, a life lived in worship as a response to God (12:1).

Again, he starts with right thinking. This thinking is not about answers to the meaning of life, the nature of the universe, or the existence of God. It is about relationships with other people, both within and outside the Christian community. In order to understand the will of God in your life, it is important to have an accurate assessment of your gifts and talents, and it is important to understand how these fit into the needs of your current situation. Your gifts are not to be used for your own advancement, but to serve the community. So, to use some management jargon, realistic self-appraisal and needs-assessment are called for.

The problem with self-appraisal is that 'self' can so often get in the way. It is easy to shore up an inflated view of our own importance by over-estimating our capabilities, attributing our experiences of failure to the incompetence of others. Conversely, we may under-estimate or under-use our abilities because of fear of failure. This type of pseudo-humility is another common defence mechanism.

Paul here insists on 'sober judgment' (v. 3), a genuine humility that makes a person willing to be used in whatever capacity God wants in a particular situation. This is a true servant mentality, which paradoxically results in freedom from self (Romans 6:22). As we have already noted, the two great leaders in the early Church, Peter and Paul, had each in his own way miserably failed Jesus. They had learnt that failure is not something to be avoided or defended against, but something that God can transform.

Verses 9–21 are a simple blueprint for Christian living, centred on love and forgiveness. In verse 15, Paul commends something that psychologists refer to as 'accurate empathy'. This ability to enter into and share in the emotions of others is one of the hallmarks of an effective counsellor or psychotherapist, and a way that genuine love is expressed in friendship. The emphasis on forgiveness is yet again reminiscent of the Lord's Prayer. For Paul, as for Jesus, a central and distinctive component of the transformed life is the letting go of grudges and desire for revenge.

6 The glory of the Lord

2 Corinthians 3:17–18

In these verses, Paul speaks in more mystical terms about the transformation of the believer. As we noted yesterday, becoming a servant of Jesus Christ frees us to act in a Christ-like way because it frees us from self-love and fear of failure. But we are freed in other ways too. Through the action of the Spirit, we are freed to develop a *relationship* with Christ and, through this, in some sense, to see God. Paul knew, when he saw the bright light on the road to Damascus and heard the voice saying 'I am Jesus…', that he had encountered the glory of God. He came to realize the truth expressed so clearly in John's Gospel: 'Whoever has seen me has seen the Father' (John 14:9).

These two verses come at the end of a difficult passage in which Paul puts forward the idea that the Torah, given to Moses under the most glorious of circumstances, has somehow ceased to express the glory of God. The fear that had stopped people relating directly to God also stopped them from understanding the glory that is contained in the Torah. But Jesus has opened the way for a direct relationship with

God and has freed the Christian from this destructive fear of God's glory.

One way in which the New Testament explains how Jesus does this is to describe him as the image or reflection of God the Father (2 Corinthians 4:4; Colossians 1:15; Hebrews 1:3). Jesus enables us to see the essence of God's glory without being blinded by it. So Jesus is not just a great human example for us to follow. He is the way in which we can come to know God. We know that Jesus' life and death can tell us what God is like because his resurrection is the seal of God's approval. We know through our experience of Jesus that God loves us (Romans 8:39). Jesus is so like God that he can be described as his son. Yet these verses tell us that, as we look at Jesus, we too are being continually transformed to become like him. Thus we are able to apprehend, and ourselves reflect, the glory of God, definitively expressed in love for other people. In this way Jesus is truly the 'first-born among many brothers' (Romans 8:29, NIV). Our transformation makes us children of God.

Guidelines

Stir us up, O Lord,
inflame our hearts and fill us with delight:
be to us both fire and sweetness:
teach us to run to you in love.
Is it not true that many turn to you
out of the depths of their blindness?
As they draw near to you
they are filled with that light of yours
which gives us the right
to become your children.
ST AUGUSTINE OF HIPPO

FURTHER READING
Richard Tedeschi and Lawrence Calhoun, *Trauma and transformation: Growing in the aftermath of suffering* (Sage, 1995). This is a book on the psychology of

transformation, published in America and quite hard to get hold of in this country, but well worth it for those who are interested

Bernard Tickerhoof, *Paradox: The spiritual path to transformation* (Twenty-Third Publications, 2002)

Esther de Waal, *Living with Contradiction* (Canterbury Press, 1997)

Rowan Williams, *Resurrection* (DLT, 1982)

Tom Wright and Marcus Borg, *The Meaning of Jesus* (SPCK, 1999)

PSALMS 42—72 (BOOK 2)

The Psalms represent a kind of hymn book of the Jerusalem temple that grew up over many centuries in ancient Israel. Although many (but far from all) of the Psalms were later attributed to King David, modern scholars agree that this was simply a later understanding and not original. As we now have it, the Psalter is divided into five books. Here we shall be examining some of the psalms in Book 2 of the Psalter (Psalms 42—72).

The psalms contained here, as elsewhere in the Psalter, consist of different types. The most common type in the Psalter, and well represented in Book 2, is the individual lament, in which an individual complains about his lot and asks God for deliverance (for example, Psalms 42—43; 51; 55; 59; 61; 69). There are also communal laments, psalms in which the whole nation bewails some major disaster that has come upon it (for example, Psalms 44; 60), and Psalm 53 perhaps also belongs here. Hymns of praise are of differing types, but within Book 2 we find examples of psalms glorifying Zion (Psalms 46; 48), an enthronement psalm (Psalm 47) celebrating God's enthronement as king, as well as a psalm of praise relating to a harvest festival (Psalm 65). Some psalms centre on the king, and this is the case with Psalm 45, a royal marriage psalm, and Psalm 72, which sets forth the ideal of kingship. There are also the so-called wisdom psalms, and Psalm 49 is one such example, with its Job-like meditation on the suffering of the righteous and the prosperity of the wicked. Other types of psalm are also represented in Book 3 of the Psalter. Containing such a variety of moods and themes as they do, the Psalms continue to speak to men and women today in their various states and conditions.

These notes are based on the New Revised Standard Version (NRSV).

1 Thirsting for God in an alien place

Psalms 42—43

It is generally agreed that Psalms 42 and 43 originally formed a single psalm. This is supported by the common refrain found in Psalms 42:5, 11 and 43:5, the fact that Psalm 43 lacks a heading, the similarities in thought and language shared by the two psalms (for example, 42:9; 43:2), and the common lament metre (3 + 2 beats) that pervades them both. Psalms 42 and 43 constitute an 'individual lament' psalm. It appears that, for some reason, the psalmist is far away from God's temple in Jerusalem and is dwelling near the source of the River Jordan (42:6), where he lives amid an oppressive enemy and feels forsaken by God.

The psalm contained here falls naturally into three sections, each consisting of five verses and each ending with a common refrain. In the first section (42:1–5), the psalmist expresses his longing for God in vivid terms ('As a deer longs for flowing streams'), laments his current situation in which he is mocked by his fellows, who ask 'Where is your God?', and recalls nostalgically the past when he used to lead people in procession to God's temple. He feels cast down, finding the only possible glimmer of hope to lie in God himself. In the second section (42:6–11), the seriousness of the psalmist's plight is underlined: he is far from the temple in the extreme north of the country by Mount Hermon and the source of the River Jordan, where he feels overwhelmed by his troubles, but nevertheless again finds a glimmer of hope in God. In the third and final section (43:1–5), the psalmist appeals to God for deliverance and looks forward to the day when he will come again to God's temple.

The first verse of this psalm has inspired the well-known hymn 'As pants the hart for cooling streams', though the fact that the verb is in the feminine form indicates that the animal is a hind rather than a hart. In Britain, we often take water for granted and regard it as a rather boring drink, but anyone who has experienced the intense heat of a Palestinian summer soon learns to appreciate its refreshing quality.

This psalm challenges us to long for the presence of God with a similar intensity. The way to this presence is through constant prayer.

2 Disaster has come upon the nation

Psalm 44

Psalm 44 is a 'communal lament' psalm, bewailing some serious military disaster that has come upon the Israelite nation. Other examples of this type of psalm include Psalms 60; 74; 79 and 137. Psalms belonging to this genre were recited on some national day of fasting and lamentation. Unlike some psalms of this type, it is not possible to be certain of the precise event that gave rise to this psalm. Suggestions include one of the disasters leading up to or including the end of the kingdom of Judah (between 609 and 586BC), or some earlier event, like the Assyrian King Sennacherib's invasion of Judah in 701BC. The older view that it reflected some disaster in the second century BC, when the Jewish Maccabean heroes were battling for freedom from their foreign overlords, is now recognized to be incorrect—the date is too late. However, whatever the original event, the language of the psalm was general enough for it to be used in connection with later disasters. Although this is a communal lament, the psalmist speaks in the first person singular in verses 4, 6 and 15: it is not clear whether this reflects the king or other national leader, or denotes simply any Israelite identifying with the fate of the nation.

The psalm's structure is clearly identifiable. The psalmist begins by recalling God's mighty acts in the earlier history of the nation (vv. 1–3), and these provide a basis for his confidence in God (vv. 4–8). We then come to the lament proper in verses 9–26. Within this section, verses 9–16 complain that God has rejected his people and has not gone out with their armies; he is scattering them among the nations and making them a laughing-stock. There follow a few verses (vv. 17–22) expressing a sense of perplexity and protest at the events that have come upon them, for the psalmist claims that they have not broken God's covenant. Finally, in verses 23–26, the psalmist appeals in desperation to God to act and deliver his people: God is, quite bluntly, told to wake up!

Most of us are probably not accustomed to expressing our feelings to God as frankly and outspokenly as the ancient Israelites. Indeed, it is interesting to note that, while psalms have often influenced Christian hymns, this is very much less so in the case of the lament psalms, especially the communal laments. Whether or not we do it in the same way as the ancient Israelites, it is important that we should feel able to share our deepest concerns with God in prayer. Even our Lord went to his death with the words of a lament psalm on his lips (the individual lament, Psalm 22).

3 A royal marriage psalm

Psalm 45

Psalm 45 celebrates the marriage between one of the kings of Judah (who were descended from King David) and his consort. As such, it is unique, constituting the only royal marriage psalm in the entire Psalter. It has sometimes been supposed that the wife is a foreign princess from Tyre in Phoenicia (modern Lebanon) on the basis of verse 12, where the Hebrew literally reads 'the daughter of Tyre will seek your favour with gifts'. It is widely agreed, however, that 'the daughter of Tyre' means 'the people of Tyre' (so NRSV; compare the common occurrence of 'the daughter of Zion' for 'the people of Zion' elsewhere in the Old Testament), so this is not a reference to the princess. Probably this psalm was used repeatedly at royal weddings in Jerusalem.

After the exile, when there was no longer a king on the throne, the psalm was eschatologized—that is, projected into the future as a description of the Messiah. Hence it is that, in the New Testament, Hebrews 1:8–9 applies the language of Psalm 45:6–7 to Christ. The former verse, 'Your throne, O God, endures for ever and ever', was understood in this New Testament passage to represent words addressed to Christ, who is held to be divine. But how could these words have been applied to the ancient kings of Judah, who do not seem to have been thought of as literally divine? Scholars get round this problem either by translating the Psalms passage differently (for example, RSV's 'Your divine throne endures for ever and ever') or by supposing that referring to the king as God is hyperbolical language, just as we use language hyperbolically when we sing 'may the king live for ever' at coronations nowadays.

The Old Testament holds marriage in high regard, and the book called the Song of Songs positively abounds in sexual imagery. Not for the Old Testament the denigration of sex that has sometimes afflicted the Christian Church. Because of this high evaluation of marriage, the New Testament can speak metaphorically of the Church as the bride of Christ (compare Ephesians 5:25). Such an understanding was presumably in mind when Hebrews 1:8–9 applied the language of Psalm 45:6–7 to Christ.

4 Zion, city of our God

Psalms 46 and 48

These two psalms are best taken together, as they both represent examples of the subcategory of hymns (or psalms of praise) known as Zion psalms. Both express the confidence that although foreign nations come to attack Jerusalem, Yahweh, the God of Israel, will intervene to deliver this, his holy city. The prophet Isaiah appealed to this tradition in 701BC, when the Assyrian King Sennacherib besieged Jerusalem, though Isaiah emphasized the need for faith in God in this connection. At a later date, however, the prophet Jeremiah criticized as superstitious the notion that God's temple in Jerusalem was inviolable (Jeremiah 7:4), and eventually Jerusalem did fall (in 586BC) to the Babylonian armies of King Nebuchadrezzar.

These psalms make use of mythological imagery to describe God's dwelling in Jerusalem. For example, in Psalm 46:4 we read, 'There is a river whose streams make glad the city of God, the holy habitation of the Most High.' There is no literal river in Jerusalem, though there is the Gihon spring, and this seems to have had mythical overtones associated with the god El, who is said to dwell on a mountain at the source of the rivers in Canaanite mythology, and with whom Yahweh, the God of Israel, was identified. Again, Psalm 48:2 speaks of Jerusalem as 'in the far north', but this is better rendered 'in the heights of Zaphon', Zaphon being the name of the Canaanite god Baal's dwelling place in Syria. This was perhaps a way of indicating that Zion was the place where true divinity dwelt—that what the Canaanites attributed to Mount Zaphon in Syria was in reality true of Jerusalem.

Although some still go on pilgrimages to sacred places, Christians (unlike the ancient Israelites) no longer associate God's presence with a particular earthly city: for the Christian, our Jerusalem is in heaven above. But we should still have the unshakeable confidence in God, come hell or high water, that these psalms express.

5 God has become king

Psalm 47

Psalm 47 is commonly described as an enthronement psalm (a subcategory of the hymns or psalms of praise), as are Psalms 93 and 96–99. It relates to Yahweh's enthronement as king, a theme central to the worship of the autumnal Feast of Tabernacles. This seems more natural than the assumption that it simply refers to God's eternal kingship, since verse 5 describes an action rather than a state: 'God has gone up with a shout, the Lord with the sound of a ram's horn' (Hebrew *shofar* means 'ram's horn', not 'trumpet', contrary to many translations, including NRSV). Identical language is used in 2 Samuel 6:15 in connection with the ark of the covenant's ascent into Jerusalem in the time of David. It seems that Psalm 47 envisages an ascent of the ark, symbolizing Yahweh's presence, up to Yahweh's cherubim throne in the holy of holies in the temple (compare Psalm 24:7–10). This would have symbolized Yahweh's assumption of kingship, verse 8 being rendered 'God has become king over the nations', not simply 'God is king over the nations'. With this would have come God's universal rule over the nations, and hence all nations, not just Israel, are called to show their joy and praise God (vv. 1, 7). Verse 9 reads, 'The princes of the peoples gather as the people of the God of Abraham. For the shields of the earth belong to God; he is highly exalted.' This relates to the theme of God's universal rule, since we recall from Genesis 12:3 that all nations were to experience the divine blessing through Abraham's descendants.

The New Testament regards this as having found fulfilment in Christ. Indeed, the coming of the kingdom of God, celebrated in this psalm, was central to the teaching of Jesus. Compare Revelation 11:15–17, 'The kingdom of the world has become the kingdom of our Lord and of his Messiah, and he will reign for ever and ever... for you have taken your great power and begun to reign.' It is not surprising that, in the Christian Church, Psalm 47 has been read in connection with Ascension day.

6 The righteous suffer and the wicked prosper

Psalm 49

Psalm 49 is commonly categorized as a wisdom psalm. That is to say, it shares some of the characteristic language of the so-called wisdom books (Proverbs, Job, Ecclesiastes) and also some of their theological concerns. In particular, it is rather Job-like in that the psalmist feels he is innocent and suffering unjustly while his wicked oppressors prosper. (Comparable wisdom psalms are Psalms 37 and 73.) Unlike Job, however, who is eventually vindicated in this life (Job 42), the psalmist has confidence that he will be vindicated by God in the afterlife, whereas the wicked will come to their doom. Compare the psalmist's words in verse 15, 'But God will ransom my soul from the power of Sheol, for he will receive me.' Psalm 73:24 probably expresses a rather similar expectation of vindication in the afterlife. We have here two of the earliest references to a more blessed afterlife, advancing beyond the earlier notion found in the Old Testament that everyone goes to Sheol, a shadowy underworld akin to the Greek concept of Hades.

Christians too should see this life in the light of eternity. As Paul says in Romans 8:18, 38–39, 'I consider that the sufferings of this present time are not worth comparing with the glory about to be revealed to us... For I am convinced that neither death, nor life, nor angels, nor rulers, nor things present, nor things to come, nor powers, nor height, nor depth, nor anything else in all creation, will be able to separate us from the love of God in Christ Jesus our Lord.'

Guidelines

Many years ago, I once asked Rowan Williams what he preached (we'd been students together at Cambridge), and he gave me the rather striking answer, 'Life is hell but God is there!' In a way, this might be said to sum up the message of some of the psalms we have been reading this week. We may feel depressed and separated from God, like the psalmist in Psalms 42—43, we may feel that life is unfair, like the author of Psalm 49, or we may feel distressed about the state of our nation, like the writer of Psalm 44, but God is always there, ever willing to listen as we pour out our hearts to him.

1 A covenant renewal psalm

Psalm 50

Psalm 50 is an interesting psalm. It appears to give us a glimpse of a covenant renewal ceremony in the context of pre-exilic Jerusalem worship, very probably at the Feast of Tabernacles at the time of the Israelite new year. This covenant renewal festival would have recapitulated the events of God's covenant-making with Israel in the time of Moses, described in the book of Exodus (see Exodus 19; 20; 24). Thus, God's coming in fire and tempest in verse 3 echoes God's manifestation in the storm in Exodus 19, and the reference to the making of a covenant by sacrifice in verse 5 echoes the ratification of the covenant on Mount Sinai described in Exodus 24. Furthermore, verses 16 onwards echo the terms of the covenant, the ten commandments of Exodus 20, which Israel was obliged to obey (compare the specific references to theft and adultery in verses 17–18).

In the middle of the psalm, God alludes to false concepts of sacrifice. Unlike some of the gods of the heathen, Yahweh the God of Israel is not one who needs to be fed by his worshippers. The reader will find a marvellous exposure of such pagan notions of sacrifice in the short book of Bel and the Dragon, an ancient detective story contained in the Apocrypha.

Just as the ancient Israelites renewed their covenant allegiance to God at the time of the new year, people in the modern world often make new year resolutions. However, we can renew our commitment to God at any time, not simply the new near, for God is a forgiving God, always willing to renew his relationship with us if we turn to him in sincere faith and repentance. Let us therefore renew our commitment to him now.

2 Create in me a clean heart, O God

Psalm 51

This is one of the profoundest psalms in the Psalter. The psalmist pleads for forgiveness from God for some grave sin that he has committed. This sin is so serious that he feels that no sacrifice can possibly atone for it. In the famous words of verse 17, the psalmist declares, 'The sacrifice acceptable to God is a broken spirit; a broken and contrite heart, O God, you will not despise.' Like so many of the individual lament psalms, we do not know the precise situation of the psalmist, but a later editor has added the words of the heading ascribing the psalm to King David, when the prophet Nathan came and confronted him in God's name with his adultery with Bathsheba and conspiracy to murder her husband, Uriah the Hittite (compare 2 Samuel 12:1–15). The psalm is certainly eminently suitable for such an occasion, even though this was doubtless not the original context.

A later, presumably exilic, editor has added the words at the very end of the psalm (vv. 18–19), implying that sacrifice would later be offered in Jerusalem after the rebuilding of Jerusalem's walls. This mundane comment rather undercuts the profound message of the earlier part of the psalm, where the psalmist feels that no sacrifice, only God's grace, can blot out his grave sin.

This psalm is highly appropriate for Christians even today to recite if they feel in particular need of forgiveness and the need to throw themselves on to God's grace. Let us make our own the prayer of verse 10: 'Create in me a clean heart, O God, and put a new and right spirit within me.'

3 Fools say in their hearts, 'There is no God'

Psalm 53

This psalm is a duplicate of Psalm 14, with some variations. Its repetition testifies to the fact that it was originally part of two different psalm collections as well as to the popularity of the psalm. The precise category to which this psalm belongs is uncertain. Overall it is perhaps safest to regard it as a kind of communal lament. The psalm is in the characteristic lament metre (3 beats + 2 beats), contains a complaint against those 'who eat up my people as they eat bread' (v. 4), and contains a plea for deliverance of Israel in verse 6.

The structure of the psalm may be outlined as follows. Verses 1–4 complain about the fools who disregard God and their consequent immoral behaviour, including 'eating up' God's people; and surprise is expressed at their lack of understanding. The mood then changes in verses 5–6, with verse 5 referring to the judgment that will come upon the ungodly, and verse 6 expressing the desire for deliverance for Israel.

Verse 1 declares, 'Fools say in their hearts, "There is no God."' It is generally held that this refers to practical rather than theoretical atheism, since the existence of the latter in ancient Israel is doubtful. It probably refers to those who doubted that there was any truly effective deity or deities behind the world, to whom they were accountable for their actions, and acted accordingly. Admittedly, there are in today's world those who truly doubt the existence of God but nevertheless live by a high moral code. There are also many in today's world who profess to believe in God but whose actions testify that they are, in effect, practical atheists. Christians everywhere should be noted for the high moral quality of their lives: as the old saying has it, 'Actions speak louder than words!'

4 Give ear to my prayer, O God!

Psalm 55

Psalm 55 is a rather long individual lament psalm. Occasionally it has been regarded as a communal lament, but this is unjustified. Again, it has sometimes been supposed that it contains two psalms (vv. 1–18 and 19–23), but most scholars consider it to be a literary unity. There are no clear indications as to the date of the psalm, even as to whether it is pre- or post-exilic.

In this psalm, the psalmist complains about enemies, utters imprecations on them, but is finally confident that God will deliver him. As is so often the case in individual lament psalms, it is not clear exactly what the psalmist is complaining about, but at one point it appears that the enemy is some familiar friend who has turned against the psalmist (vv. 12–14). The imprecations on enemies that we find in this psalm (compare vv. 15, 23) will disturb the modern, sensitive reader. Such imprecations are not unknown in other lament psalms. These sentiments certainly fall short of the Christian ideal of loving one's enemies, and need not be defended simply because they are found in scripture. The psalmists, after all, were only human. Further, we need to recall that for much of the Old Testament period there was no meaningful afterlife belief, so many psalmists felt that if justice was to be done, it had to be done in this world, and they were understandably impatient to see it come to pass.

Two passages of this psalm in particular have become well known through later citation. First, Mendelssohn's famous song 'O for the wings of a dove' is based on Psalm 55:6–8, where the psalmist declares, 'And I say, "O that I had wings like a dove! I would fly away and be at rest; truly, I would flee away; I would lodge in the wilderness; I would hurry to find a shelter for myself from the raging wind and tempest."' Second, the words of verse 22, 'Cast your burden on the Lord, and he will sustain you' are echoed in 1 Peter 5:7: 'Cast all your anxiety on him, because he cares for you.' Together these two passages continue to provide deep spiritual guidance for the believer today.

5 Deliver me from my enemies, O my God!

Psalm 59

This psalm is in the form of an individual lament, in that the subject is spoken of in the first person singular ('I', 'me'). However, the enemies appear not to be local Israelites, as in so many other individual laments, but rather foreign nations (vv. 5, 8), as is the case in communal laments. It is plausible to suppose that we can explain this situation by envisaging the subject of the psalm as the Israelite king or possibly some other representative of the nation—for example, an army commander—though conceivably any individual could be identifying himself with the fate of the nation. The setting given in the psalm's heading (relating it to Saul's attempt on David's life in 1 Samuel 19:11–17) is certainly a later editorial addition, as in comparable Psalms like 52; 56; 57 and 60.

The structure of the psalm is rather unusual compared with that of many other laments. It seems to consist of two parts, verses 1–10 and verses 11–17, each of which contains a lament to God in the first half (vv. 1–5, 11–13), followed by variants on a refrain (vv. 6–7, 14–15), and concluding with a thanksgiving section in which the psalmist looks forward to deliverance (vv. 8–10, 16–17), the latter parts of each having certain similarities (vv. 9–10, 17). The change of mood at the end of each section is paralleled in some other individual lament psalms in which the psalmist ends on a hopeful note. This type of mood change has often been attributed by scholars to the intervention of a salvation oracle given by a priest in between the lament and thanksgiving sections. There is no proof of this, however, and it is perhaps more natural to suppose that the mood change is attributable to the confidence that often comes to those who pour out their souls in faith to God. We too, if we continue praying steadfastly in faith to God, will be rewarded with the confidence that our prayers have been heard.

6 O God, you have rejected us!

Psalm 60

This psalm is clearly a communal lament, bewailing as it does some great disaster that has come upon the nation. (Part of this psalm, vv. 5–12, is repeated in Psalm 108:6–13.) The psalm falls into three sections. In the first part (vv. 1–5), the psalmist complains that God in his anger has rejected his people and brought distress upon the nation. In consequence, he prays for God to rescue them. In the second section (vv. 6–8), we have a divine oracle in which God himself speaks, emphasizing his lordship over Israel and Judah, as well as over Edom, Moab and Philistia. The third and final section is in verses 9–12. Here the psalmist continues the lament, complaining that God does not go out with their armies, and appeals for help against the enemy. In the final verse (v. 12), he expresses the confidence that with God they will be victorious over their foes.

Such a psalm, like others of this type (for instance, Psalms 44; 74; 79 and 137), would have been recited on some national day of fasting. It is not possible to be certain precisely what national calamity is being lamented here; the details in the heading relating to David's campaigns against Aram (Syria) and Edom reflect later interpretation. Verse 6 implies that the northern kingdom of Israel is under foreign rule, signifying a date after its fall in 722BC. Possibly the psalm refers to the fall of the southern kingdom of Judah in 586BC: this could explain the mention of Edom in verse 9, for the Edomites supported the Babylonians in some way when they conquered Judah (compare Psalm 137:7–9; and Obadiah).

Guidelines

With the exception of the covenant renewal Psalm 50, the psalms this week are lament psalms of one type or another. With the exception of Psalm 51, however, in all of these the psalmist pleads with God for deliverance from enemies, whether individual or communal, and has confidence that God will answer his prayer. Most of us today are probably not afflicted with enemies in the way that the ancient psalmists were. Nevertheless, we too all have our own problems and concerns which we can bring to God in prayer.

1 God is my refuge

Psalm 61

This is another individual lament psalm. The psalmist pleads to God for help and protection against the enemy (v. 3), but it is not possible to be more precise about his exact circumstances. Doubtless the language is deliberately vague, thus making the psalm applicable to a wider circle of supplicants than would have been possible if it had been too precise.

The attribution of the psalm to David is traditional. Some scholars have, nevertheless, interpreted it as a royal psalm because of the explicit prayer for the king in verses 6–7, while others have seen these verses as an interpolation. Neither supposition is necessary, however, since intercessions for the king are sometimes included in comparable Babylonian lament psalms prayed by ordinary individuals. Presumably the king here prayed for is the Israelite king of David's line, in which case the psalm will date from before the exile.

The psalmist seeks refuge in God, and some interesting images for the divine protection are to be found in verses 2–4. Thus, in verse 2 the psalmist seeks refuge in 'the rock that is higher than I'. It has sometimes been suggested that this refers to the sacred rock now enclosed in the Muslim mosque known as the Dome of the Rock in Jerusalem, which probably constituted the site of the holy of holies in the ancient Jerusalem temple, above which God's immanent presence was believed to be enthroned on the cherubim. However, since God is directly spoken of as a rock elsewhere in the psalms, this is probably simply a metaphor for God himself, comparable to the reference to God as 'a strong tower' in the next verse (v. 3).

Again, the psalmist's wish to 'find refuge under the shelter of your wings' (v. 4) has sometimes been seen as an allusion to the wings of the cherubim (winged sphinxes)—the throne above the ark of the covenant in the holy of holies where God's immanent presence was believed to be centred. Yet again, however, we probably have to do rather with metaphorical imagery, God being envisaged as akin to a watchful mother bird (compare Deuteronomy 32:11). This imagery is frequent in the psalms (see Psalms 17:8; 36:7; 57:1; 63:7; 91:4).

Like the ancient psalmist, we too can make God our refuge and have his presence with us through all the multifarious experiences of life.

2 You visit the earth and water it

This is a hymn (psalm of praise) that falls naturally into three sections. In the first (vv. 1–4), God in Zion is praised as the one who answers the prayers of his people and bestows forgiveness and blessing. In the second (vv. 5–8), we read of God's power as creator and saviour: as creator, he subdues the chaos waters and fashions the earth; and as saviour, he subdues the powers of chaos as they reassert themselves in the historical sphere in the form of hostile nations. In the third and final section (vv. 9–13), we have a most beautiful hymn of praise extolling God for bringing rain to the earth, which results in fertility for the world and a most bounteous harvest.

This psalm gives every impression of having had its setting at one of ancient Israel's harvest festivals. Scholars disagree, however, as to whether this was at the time of the Feast of Unleavened Bread, Weeks (Pentecost) or Tabernacles.

Israel is a land very much dependent on the rain for its fertility. Unlike in Britain, where rain can come at any time and people tend to grumble about having too much of it, in Israel the rainy season is limited to the period between October and April. (The Old Testament speaks of the former and latter rains, though in fact it rains on and off throughout this period.) The other half of the year (April till October) is a long, hot and dry season, though not a barren one, since this is when many of the crops ripen, provided the rains have come during the previous autumn and winter. Famine results if the rains have failed to come (see the Joseph story in Genesis). The crucial importance of the rain explains why the Israelites were so frequently tempted to worship the Canaanite god Baal, whose special sphere of activity was believed to be the bringing of rain and fertility. Baal was called 'rider of the clouds', and this imagery is appropriated to Yahweh, the God of Israel, in verse 11, where the psalmist declares, 'Your wagon [or chariot] tracks overflow with richness.'

3 Let the peoples praise you, O God!

Psalm 67

This short and cheerful psalm opens in verse 1 with the prayer, 'May God be gracious to us and bless us, and make his face to shine upon us.' These words echo part of the so-called priestly benediction of Numbers 6:24–26, 'The Lord bless you and keep you; the Lord make his face to shine upon you, and be gracious to you; the Lord lift up his countenance upon you, and give you peace.' To a remarkable extent, this psalm is pervaded by the call for all nations—not simply Israel—to praise, rejoice in and revere God. This is found not only in the refrain repeated in verses 3 and 5, 'Let the peoples praise you, O God; let all the peoples praise you', but also in verse 4 and the second half of verse 7. Accordingly, a full half of the psalm is concerned with the call to the nations of the world to worship Yahweh, the God of Israel.

Although, in the post-exilic period, the Jews succeeded in making a number of converts to Judaism (called 'proselytes') from among the Gentiles—and it is from this period that the psalm probably derives—it was only with the coming of Christianity, which started as a messianic sect within Judaism, that the worship of the God of Israel truly spread to all nations. It is accordingly appropriate that this psalm (commonly known by its Latin name, the *Deus misereatur*) appears in the Anglican service of Evening Prayer (as an alternative to the *Nunc Dimittis*) in response to the New Testament lesson.

It is because of verse 6 that this psalm has sometimes been regarded as a harvest psalm (like Psalm 65, considered above), as in the NRSV's translation, 'The earth has yielded its increase; God, our God, has blessed us'. Certainly the Hebrew word rendered 'increase' usually refers to the agricultural produce of the land. However, since the second half of verse 6 (and similarly verse 7) is certainly to be rendered either in the future tense ('God, our God, will bless us') or as a wish ('May God, our God, bless us'), it is more natural to translate the first half of verse 6 either as 'The earth will yield its increase' (prophetic perfect) or as 'May the earth yield its increase' (precative perfect), which does not suit a harvest festival.

4 A processional psalm

This is a very long and sometimes obscure psalm, the latter point probably being a sign of its antiquity. It perhaps dates from the period of the united kingdom under Solomon (compare the reference to tribes from both north and south participating in worship, in verse 27). Thematically it belongs to the same circle of ideas as Psalm 47 and other psalms concerned with God's enthronement as king (for example, Psalms 93 and 96–99), which had their setting at the autumnal Feast of Tabernacles: verses 24–25 refer to a procession associated with Yahweh as king, and this seems to have involved a procession with the ark of the covenant. The presence of the ark is supported by verse 1, words elsewhere associated with the ark in Numbers 10:35, and by the allusion to God's ascent to the sanctuary in verses 17–18 (compare Psalms 24:7–10; 47:5).

While accompanying a procession with the ark, the psalm celebrates the victories and saving acts of God towards Israel in its past history. Verse 6 probably alludes to the exodus from Egypt ('he leads the prisoners to prosperity'); verses 7–10 allude to God's manifestation (theophany) at Mount Sinai and Israel's wanderings in the wilderness; and verses 11–14 make reference to God's victory over certain kings, reflecting most probably Israel's defeat of Sisera and his cohorts described in Judges 5. The psalm then goes on to speak of the envy of the mountain of Bashan (probably Mount Hermon) towards God's choice of Mount Zion (Jerusalem) for his sanctuary, and verses 17–18 to describe God's ascent thither. God having ascended his throne, the psalm goes on to anticipate his future victory over all enemies (vv. 21–23) and his universal rule over all nations (vv. 28–32).

The psalmist's vision of God's kingdom coming over the world, subduing all the powers of evil beneath it, is one that Christians share. However, the psalmist sometimes expresses this vision rather crudely in terms of military victory over enemies, in a way that modern Christian readers will find distasteful (compare v. 23). The New Testament encourages us to spiritualize this imagery when it says that 'our struggle is not against enemies of blood and flesh, but... against the spiritual forces of evil in the heavenly places' (Ephesians 6:12).

5 Save me, O God—the waters are up to my neck!

Psalm 69

Psalm 69 is a particularly long example of the commonest type of psalm in the Psalter, the individual lament psalm, in which an individual bewails his lot to God and pleads for deliverance. Several of the characteristic features of the individual laments are found here—for example, the plea for help (vv. 1, 13–18), the description of the misery endured by the psalmist (vv. 2–4), and curses directed against the enemies (vv. 22–31). The psalmist complains of those who hate him without cause, seek to destroy him and attack him with lies (v. 4). This situation is described as sinking into the waters (vv. 1–2, 15): this reflects belief in the watery nature of the underworld (Sheol). The curses towards the end of the psalm (vv. 22–31) will offend the modern Christian and, indeed, any sensitive reader. However, without condoning them (they fall short of the Christian ideal of loving one's enemies), we should try to understand these human sentiments: they doubtless reflect an experience of acute suffering.

This psalm is noteworthy for the number of times it is quoted or echoed in the New Testament (compare v. 4 with John 15:25; v. 9 with John 2:17; Romans 15:3; vv. 22–23 with Romans 11:9 - 10; v. 24 with Revelation 16:1; v. 25 with Acts 1:20; v. 28 with Revelation 3:5; 13:8; 17:8; 20:12, 15; 21:27). In addition, although it is not explicitly quoted, verse 21 ('They gave me poison for food, and for my thirst they gave me vinegar to drink') appears to be echoed in Jesus' passion narrative (Mark 15:36; Matthew 27:34, 48; Luke 23:36; John 19:29). It seems, in fact, that like another individual lament psalm (Psalm 22), Psalm 69 was understood by the early Christians as prefiguring the passion of Christ.

6 The ideal king

Psalm 72

Psalm 72 is clearly one of the royal psalms (although the attribution to Solomon in the heading is simply later tradition). It presents an ideal picture of what the kings of David's line should be like—ruling justly and peacefully over the world, with a special concern for the poor and needy. It is a noble ideal. None of the Israelite kings really lived up to this ideal so, after the exile, when there was no longer an Israelite king on the throne and the Jews were subject to rule by foreign nations, the idealized picture here came to be ascribed to the future Messiah, who would make the ideal a reality. For example, verse 8 ('May he have dominion from sea to sea, and from the River to the ends of the earth') is taken up and applied to the Messiah in Zechariah 9:10, where we read, 'His dominion shall be from sea to sea, and from the River to the ends of the earth'. The previous verse in Zechariah, 9:9, which speaks of the Messiah riding on an ass, is of course applied to Jesus in the New Testament (Mark 11:1–10, and equivalent passages).

It is also possible to hear echoes of Psalm 72:15 ('May gold of Sheba be given to him') in the story of the magi in Matthew 2:11, where gold, in addition to frankincense and myrrh, is brought to the infant Jesus. It is therefore not surprising that a whole Christian hymn is based on this psalm—the well-known 'Jesus shall reign where'er the sun'.

Christians look for the coming of God's kingdom ('Thy kingdom come') and see Jesus Christ as the Messiah who brings in this kingdom. It is our role as Christians to let Jesus rule in our own lives and to seek to establish his rule over all things in the world.

Guidelines

In this final week of readings from Book 2 of the Psalter, there has been not so much lament and a bit more praise than in the previous two weeks. This is even more true of the second half of the Psalter, especially Psalms 100—150, for it has often been observed that overall the Psalter moves from a greater emphasis on lament in the first half to a greater emphasis on praise in the second. Although petition to God is a crucial part of prayer, it is not good if this is all that our prayers consist of. There are so many things that we should thank and praise God for. Let us ponder all the good things of life that we experience, and thank and praise him for them now.

FURTHER READING

Arnold A. Anderson, *Psalms* (2 vols.), New Century Bible Commentary (Oliphants, 1972)

Bernhard W. Anderson, *Out of the Depths: The Psalms Speak for Us Today* (Westminster, 1983)

John Day, *Psalms*, Old Testament Guides (Sheffield Academic Press, 1990)

Patrick D. Miller, *Interpreting the Psalms* (Fortress Press, 1986)

Klaus Seybold, *Introducing the Psalms* (T&T Clark, 1990)

THE WRITINGS OF LUKE
(PART 3)

Over the next four weeks, we shall be reading from the final chapters of Luke's Gospel and Acts. In Acts, Paul is in Jerusalem, on trial before Jewish and Roman authorities. In the Gospel, Jesus too is in Jerusalem, facing the same authorities. The verdicts are different. Paul is deemed innocent of the charges brought against him and despatched to Rome to appear before the emperor. Jesus is found guilty and crucified. Paul's journey to Rome is perilous but, once there, he continues his ministry untroubled, in the place from which the gospel will eventually reach 'the ends of the earth'. Jesus endures a humiliating death, his faith in God tested yet undiminished, his promise vindicated by the resurrection on the third day.

The notes explore the connections between the stories of Paul and Jesus, with their themes of passion and vindication. They are based on the Revised Standard Version, though they can be used with any version of the Bible.

Paul before the authorities

At the previous hearing before the Jewish council in Jerusalem (Acts 23:1ff), Paul's remarks caused a riot and he was taken into the protective custody that eventually brought him to Caesarea, where we pick up the story once more.

1 The ringleader of a sect

Acts 24:1–9

Paul now stands before the Roman governor Felix, who was in charge of Palestine from AD52 to 60. The high priest Ananias, a powerful man in the Jewish community, had presided over the proceedings last time.

Now he comes to present his case before the emperor's representative, accompanied by a few Jewish leaders and Tertullus, their spokesman. His opening words, with their fulsome flattery, are no more than a contemporary leader would expect in a speech like this.

The substance of the accusation against Paul is part fact, part fiction. Verse 5 shows how Paul was perceived by the Jewish leadership. He is associated with a branch of the Jesus movement (the Hellenists) whose loyalty to the temple and the law of Moses is questionable. His conviction that Gentiles and Jews belong to God's covenant community on the same basis has made him a public peril, a lethal contaminant and a threat to law and order. Moreover, he is but the ringleader of a dangerous and subversive movement. The language could hardly be more frightening. It is calculated to unsettle Felix, whose period of office was marked by rising Jewish unrest. Verse 6, as we have already seen, is not true (21:29), but such were the more traditionalist Jewish feelings towards Paul that it was all too easy to misconstrue the presence in the temple of one whose associations with Gentiles were well known (21:28–29).

There are multiple motives behind this blend of fact and fiction. The Nazarenes are seen as one more Jewish sect, competing with others for the soul of Israel. Ananias and the Sanhedrin are asserting their authority as the true leaders of God's people and guardians of their venerable traditions. But the high priest remains in office only by imperial permission. These Jewish leaders cannot afford too much unrest among their own people if they want to preserve their position.

There is no love lost where Paul is concerned. There is too much at stake. Is this why Paul had appealed to the emperor? Did he think that was the only way to get a fair hearing? With strong feelings playing such a big part in the proceedings, the importance of viewing things from a distance is obvious.

2 The Way is not a sect

Acts 24:10–22

Paul addresses the charges in reverse order. He rejects any suggestion that he was the instigator of trouble in the temple, and later implies that his accusers' evidence is second-hand (vv. 19, 20). But he makes no attempt to deny his involvement in 'the Way'. This name is first used for the Jesus movement in 9:2, which introduces the account of Paul's journey to Damascus. Interestingly, the Essenes also referred to themselves as 'the Way', and they had links with Damascus. Is 'the Way' another Jewish sect, like the Pharisees, the Essenes and the Sadducees? Paul's '...which they call a sect' (v. 14) suggests a more daring interpretation of those who follow the Nazarene.

Paul claims to be utterly loyal to Israel's ancestral traditions. The God he worships is 'the God of our fathers'. The touchstone of his faith is 'the law... (and) the prophets'. As one schooled by the Pharisees, he shares the Jewish hope in 'a resurrection of both the just and the unjust', though not all Jews believed this. It was a relative newcomer to Israel's faith, appearing for the first time in Daniel 12:2 (most scholars date this around 160BC). Jesus had entered into the debates over the resurrection of the dead (Luke 20:27ff), and Paul did the same at the previous hearing in Jerusalem (Acts 23:6ff).

In what sense is Paul on trial 'with respect to the resurrection of the dead' (v. 21)? His introduction of this idea in 23:6 might have seemed opportunistic, an attempt to divide and rule. But as a follower of Jesus, the resurrection of the dead has become the kernel of his faith. Luke is fond of depicting the resurrection and exaltation of the crucified Jesus as the precursor of the coming of the Spirit (see Acts 2:33) —and that Spirit has fallen on Jew and Gentile alike. The 'resurrection of the dead' has acquired a new meaning for those in 'the Way'. It is the basis of a restored Israel, a bigger Israel, one no longer defined by race or nationality but a truly international people whose faith in Israel's God and loyalty to Israel's scriptures have been reshaped by the impact of Jesus.

Paul claims that his involvement in 'the Way' has done nothing to undermine his Jewish faith: his conscience is clear (v. 16). Is he also suggesting that 'the Way', far from being just another Jewish sect, is the true Israel? A sect might have been easier to deal with. Paul's claim that 'the Way' embodies the very soul of Israel makes him too threatening.

3 I appeal to Caesar

The hearing before Felix proves inconclusive. Paul remains in custody, though with some freedoms (v. 23). He meets regularly with the governor to discuss his faith, but Felix is more open to bribery than repentance (vv. 25–26). By the time Felix is recalled to Rome (around AD60), Paul has been under arrest for two years—unsatisfactory, we might think, but at least it keeps his opponents happy.

Festus is quick to visit Jerusalem (v. 1)—wisely, because tension there is rising. All the more reason for dealing with Paul without delay. Paul's enemies resort to old tactics (v. 3; cf. 23:12ff), but Festus is having nothing of this. Once again, Paul appears before a Roman official. The Jewish leaders are more menacing than ever: they 'stood about him' (v. 7). This time, Paul includes a reference to Caesar alongside his earlier protestations: perhaps he is being accused of political subversion. Festus, new to the job, seems willing to meet the Jews halfway and offers Paul the option of standing trial in Jerusalem. But Paul knows that his only chance of a fair hearing lies in his appeal to Caesar—the right of every Roman citizen.

Once again, Paul is shunted between Jerusalem and Rome (as was Jesus; see Luke 23:6–16). But Luke continues to give the impression that Rome is prepared to protect Paul from his Jewish enemies, without being particularly sympathetic to his cause. It may have been important for Luke to present Roman authority in a good light, for the sake of those in his audience who would question the wisdom of joining a movement whose founder was crucified by the Romans. Like Jesus, Paul is innocent in Roman eyes (three times Pilate declared that, in his opinion, Jesus did not deserve to be executed; see Luke 23:4, 14, 22). If Rome has nothing to fear from 'the Way', the followers of Jesus can take heart from Paul's treatment.

In the volatile atmosphere of Jerusalem, concerns about Jewish identity and the distinctive place of Israel in the world inevitably make Paul's attitudes to Moses and the temple difficult to swallow. His mission has made a creative thinker of him. He has been bold enough to redefine the fundamentals of his once very traditional faith, in the light of the resurrection of Jesus from the dead and the outpouring of the Spirit on Jews and Gentiles alike. His experience reminds us that his successors in every age must expect to draw anger as well as appreciation from their audiences.

4 Nothing deserving death

Acts 25:13–27

Agrippa is the son of the Herod in Acts 12, and the grandson of Herod the Great. When his father died (AD44), Agrippa was only seventeen, and the emperor at the time (Claudius) was unwilling to delegate authority over the whole of his father's province to him. Gradually, though, Agrippa was given more and more Jewish territory. Here, with his sister and consort Bernice, he takes the opportunity to welcome Festus, who loses no time in trying to resolve the situation he has inherited from his rather dilatory predecessor. If he is to send Paul for trial in Rome, he needs to fashion a charge against him. Perhaps Agrippa can help: he had a reputation for representing Jewish causes in Rome. We are reminded of the way Pontius Pilate sought the assistance of Agrippa's uncle (Herod Antipas, client king of Galilee) to reach a decision about Jesus (Luke 23:6ff).

Notice Festus' assessment of the issues surrounding Paul (v. 19). They are purely Jewish concerns, associated with Jesus. The chief priests are at odds with Paul 'about their own superstition'. The term is not as negative as the translation suggests. A *superstitio* is a local or national religion; from a Roman perspective, the religion of the Jews is one among many found throughout the empire. Paul and his opponents are divided by matters of opinion: Jesus is 'dead', though 'Paul asserted [him] to be alive'. Festus speaks as an outsider, reflecting the view of other Gentiles in Acts that the Jesus movement is part of Judaism (for example, the crowds in Philippi in 16:20, and the town clerk at Ephesus in 19:37ff), and assuming that the Jewish leaders speak for the whole people (v. 24).

Festus is honest enough to acknowledge his own shortcomings (v. 20)—rare, we might think, in a politician—without allowing himself to be pressured into abandoning his conviction about Paul

(vv. 24, 25). By combining detachment with determination, he turns out to be Paul's best hope for a fair trial.

5 I saw a light from heaven

Acts 26:1–17

Paul's defence before Agrippa is the third account in Acts of what happened to him on the road to Damascus (see also chs. 9 and 22). There are broad similarities but, as we might expect, distinctive emphases, particularly in this final version of events, which forms the climax of all that Paul has said publicly since chapter 21.

Paul's reference to his life as a Pharisee is unique to this account. The Pharisees had a zeal for biblical holiness, shown by their desire to apply the law of Moses to every detail of life. Some Pharisees were drawn to the Jesus movement (Acts 15:5), even though many of Jesus' most vigorous opponents were Pharisees. Here, as he did before the Sanhedrin in 23:6, Paul makes common cause with them. He sees himself on trial for the ancient and venerable Jewish hope in the resurrection of the dead, now fulfilled in Jesus the Messiah.

In verses 9–11, Paul plays up his former opposition to 'the saints' as an agent of the chief priests. But in doing so he makes it abundantly clear why they oppose him so fiercely. He is a traitor to their cause, a turncoat. We hardly need reminding that groups often reserve their most vehement opposition for someone who was formerly 'one of us'. Verses 12–18 contain some distinctive material: the heavenly light also illuminated Paul's travelling companions; the risen Christ spoke in Hebrew. 'It hurts you to kick against the goads' is a proverbial addition whose meaning is not clear. Here Paul's commission comes directly from Jesus and not through Ananias, as in the other two accounts. The wording of verse 18 echoes Isaiah 42:6–7. It is as if Paul is being called to fulfil the destiny of God's servant Israel as a light who opens the eyes of the Gentiles, just as Jesus does in Luke 4:18–21.

Paul had been travelling to Damascus 'with the authority and commission of the chief priests' (v. 12). But he encountered a higher authority, 'a light from heaven, brighter than the sun... Jesus whom you are persecuting', and a commission to continue the work that his

Lord had begun. Paul presents himself to Agrippa as both conservative and innovative—faithful to the traditions and hopes of his people, loyal to the Way of Jesus, at the leading edge of new developments in Israel. Had his mission not been so firmly anchored in heavenly authority, these contrasting forces may well have pulled him apart.

6 Not madness but the sober truth

Acts 26:19–32

In his defence, Paul claims that his controversial actions have proceeded from 'the heavenly vision'. He may have said earlier that he was on trial 'for hope…' (26:6), but as he nears the end of his speech, he is closer to the nub of the issue. That a former persecutor of the Jesus movement should become one of its most prodigious advocates is reason enough for zealous Jews to take action against him. He has asked the same of both Jews and Gentiles—repentance, the readiness to embrace Israel's God in heart, mind and action. Because of the heavenly vision, Paul can no more conceive of God apart from Jesus than he can read Moses and the prophets without seeing the suffering and resurrection of this Messiah. Israel's ancient vocation—to be light to the world—has at last been fulfilled in the one who encountered Paul as light from heaven.

Is it madness to take such a stand on the basis of a claim to divine revelation—madness to see the Way of Jesus, rather than a plethora of national 'superstitions', as salvation for all the empire's peoples? Claims to be in touch with another dimension of reality are often dismissed as madness in cultures that prize more mundane forms of rationality. This is especially true when such claims are accompanied by unusual or challenging behaviour. But Paul defends his sanity as well as his cause. Notice how he anchors his belief in the public world to which Festus and Agrippa belong. His ministry has always been open to scrutiny (v. 26). His teaching is rooted not in esoteric wisdom available only to the few, but in the scriptures, whose message is publicly available to Jews and Gentiles. Madness means being out of touch with what others take for granted as 'reality'. Paul claims to speak 'the sober truth' (v. 25): he is utterly in touch.

Does Paul touch a raw nerve in Agrippa (v. 28), or is the king just being sarcastic? Either way, he and Festus recognize sufficient truth in Paul's testimony for Festus to remain at a loss as to what to write about Paul to Caesar (25:26–27). Paul's enemies are not allowed to have the last word. A Jewish king (in the event, the last Jewish king) and a Roman governor would gladly have set Paul free.

Guidelines

Resting religious authority solely in texts, however venerable, is a risky business. Words are human, not divine, and they never have a single, fixed-for-all-time meaning. The history of interpretation has taught us that the scriptures can be read in different ways. This is why Paul and his opponents could draw different conclusions from the same body of scripture.

Sectarian groups go against the grain where words and texts are concerned, by restricting their meaning to 'the official view'. This may make sense when a group's survival is at stake. But in a bigger, more plural world, the survival of one group—however important this may be—is never enough.

The Jesus movement issued a call to move beyond mere survival and look for ways of creating a more inclusive vision of humanity. In this, the scriptures have a clear authority. But it matters how they are interpreted. With Paul, the followers of Jesus can only ever read the scriptures as members of the Way, which is not a sect but a truly international people.

Let the Way of Jesus illuminate the breadth of the vision for humanity in the scriptures, and give us the courage to resist anything that reduces God's purposes to mere survival.

Jesus in Jerusalem

Jesus began his journey to Jerusalem as far back as Luke 9:51. This journey takes up nearly half of the Gospel, providing the framework for much of Jesus' teaching about what it means to take up the cross daily and follow him. Jesus finally arrives in the city among the pilgrims who have come for Passover.

1 The time of Jerusalem's visitation

Luke 19:29–48

When Jesus arrives in the city, he is acclaimed by 'the whole multitude of the disciples' (v. 37), among them supporters and followers from Galilee. Passover pilgrims traditionally sang verses from Psalm 118 as they approached the city. Luke applies their acclamations specifically to Jesus as Israel's messianic king. What are his followers expecting from him? Those closest to Jesus have already been told that he is a 'Son of Man Messiah' (9:20–21), who will absorb the violence thrown at him by Israel's leaders and somehow use it to bring in God's kingdom. Now, for the benefit of a wider public full of expectation, he comes not in a chariot at the head of an army, but on a colt.

Jesus' concern for Jerusalem runs deep. We have heard it before: 'O Jerusalem, Jerusalem, killing the prophets and stoning those who are sent to you! How often would I have gathered your children together as a hen gathers her brood under her wings, and you would not!' (13:34). The holy city has lost its way. Its name means 'city of peace', but violence towards God's emissaries once again stalks its streets. History is about to be repeated (v. 47), and the city will reap a tragic reward (vv. 43–44 draw on descriptions of the fall of Jerusalem 600 years before, in Isaiah 29:3 and Ezekiel 4:2).

Luke's account of the so-called 'cleansing of the temple' is brief, and concentrates on the exploitation of pilgrims by those who exchange everyday money for the specially minted coinage with which the temple tax was paid, and sell unblemished animals for the sacrifices. Greed has become the new idolatry in the temple precincts and beyond (see 20:46–47). So Jesus reclaims Israel's most sacred place for its primary purpose—prayer that fosters communion with God.

Jesus has come to Jerusalem as a pilgrim and more: he sees it as 'the time of your visitation' (v. 44). In the Hebrew scriptures, this refers to God's coming to Israel in judgment or deliverance, sometimes with an opportunity for repentance. Jesus suggests that rejection of his mission will prove catastrophic. He has been advocating a different way to be God's covenant people—seeing holiness as generous, welcoming love rather than sectarian zeal. The one is able to heal the nation, and allow its holy city to be true to its name. The other thrives on the kind of violence that will eventually make Jerusalem a ruin.

2 He will give the vineyard to others

Luke 20:1–20

The Jewish leaders smell trouble. Passover is a time of celebration. The memory of liberation from foreign oppression is intoxicating. Nationalistic feelings are running high in a city full of pilgrims. The last thing the chief priests can afford is trouble. The heavy hand of Rome, which would quell any uprising, would be more unwelcome than ever at festival time. So they search for some pretext to bring Jesus before the Roman authorities, who have ways of making a public spectacle of dissidents to discourage their followers.

Jesus is too clever for their questions about his authority. A direct claim to divine authority would mean that he was asserting himself as an alternative to the chief priests, who could then present him to Pilate as a self-styled leader and a threat to public order. Denying divine authority would expose Jesus as a fraud before his followers. The reference to John the Baptist allows Jesus to turn the question back on his opponents.

A further offensive comes in the parable of the vineyard. The imagery is scriptural: Israel is God's vineyard (Isaiah 5:1–5). The practice is contemporary: absentee landlords were greatly resented for creaming off local wealth. The storyline is God's dealings with Israel narrated in the scriptures. The chosen people are given the responsibility of living faithfully before God in the world. God's messengers remind them that he has a right to the 'fruit' of his vineyard, understood as the seamless consistency of worship and social justice. The fate of the final messenger—the beloved son and heir—anticipates the violence coming to Jesus. The point of the parable is that Israel dare not take its place in the world for granted.

The chief priests realize that the story is aimed at them, as well they might. There is evidence that, at the time of Jesus, Isaiah's vineyard was interpreted as the temple. So Jesus drives home his earlier attack (19:46) and announces the end of an institution and its leadership. But there is more. The vineyard will go to others. The rejected stone will become the foundation stone of a new construction, and also an agency of divine judgment. Jesus draws on the 'stone' imagery of Psalm 118:22 (a Passover psalm), Isaiah 8:14–15 and Daniel 2:34ff— the texts are linked elsewhere in the New Testament (see 1 Peter 2:6–8) and in the Dead Sea Scrolls—to declare that Israel's future belongs with those whom its leaders reject.

They may save their own skin in the short term, but the chief priests and their associates are guilty of betraying their God-given responsibility. Jesus and his followers will recall Israel to its true vocation. Theirs will be a vineyard of the violated.

3 Caesar, Moses and David

Luke 20:21–47

The search is on for an indictable offence—or at least some way of discrediting Jesus. How loyal is he to Caesar? 'Is it *lawful* for us to give tribute to Caesar?' suggests that there is some dispute about how to interpret Moses on this issue. There is nothing in the law that applies directly, but Roman coins are inscribed with Caesar's head and the second commandment forbids making graven images (Exodus 20:4). A straight 'yes' or 'no' from Jesus will set him against one authority or another. He sees through this mischief. Israel is part of the Roman empire, and imperial currency is in circulation. The Jewish leaders benefit from judicious compromise with Rome. They should be the last to play games like this. Jesus' reply, 'Render to Caesar… and to God…', is not to separate politics and God, but to recognize that each has his due—to Caesar the taxes owed by an occupied people; to God the fruits of his vineyard. Scripture says nothing about paying taxes to a foreign ruler, but plenty about loyalty to God. Little wonder Jesus' enemies are once again silenced.

How loyal is Jesus to Moses? Many Jews, Pharisees included, now believe in the resurrection of the dead, part of the hope for a new, messianic order when the kingdom of God finally arrives. Sadducees find no place for it. As members of the Jewish aristocracy, they do quite well out of the old, established order. They justify their position by Moses' silence about resurrection, and its seeming absurdity in view of Moses' injunction about family solidarity (see Deuteronomy 25:5–6). Jesus' reply shows him to be both traditional and modern. *Modern*, in that he stands by his beliefs in the resurrection, and chastises the Sadducees for their ignorance. In the new world, marriage as they understand it—with women belonging to men as their property—will not exist. *Traditional*, in that he argues that the God of Moses is the God of the living. What, then, is the problem with resurrection of the dead? Even some of his opponents are impressed.

Now it is Jesus' turn to ask an awkward question. What kind of Messiah do the scriptures lead us to expect? Some, going back to 2 Samuel 7:12–16, give rise to the hope for a 'son of David', a warrior king who will restore the greatness of David's empire. But Psalm 110:1 (which was assumed to have been written by David and was just beginning to be interpreted as a messianic psalm) has David speaking of the Messiah as his 'Lord': 'The Lord (that is, God) said to my (David's) Lord (that is, the Messiah)…'. If the Messiah is David's Lord, David cannot provide the messianic template—something that Jesus has been insisting on all along.

The issues about authority here are complex, and they rest on ways of interpreting the scriptures that were acceptable then but less so now. But Jesus can outwit his opponents because their authority resides in texts, whereas his is rooted in his relationship with God, as the Gospel makes clear throughout. He is difficult to trap with the arguments used by his enemies, because his authority is of a different order from theirs. As we shall see, they will come to rely on other means of achieving their ambitions.

4 Watch at all times

This is Jesus' last public speech. The evangelist adapts material from Mark 13 and repeats sayings found earlier in the Gospel (vv. 8–9, compare 17:22–37; vv. 12–19, compare 12:11–12). He presents Jesus' final challenge to three audiences—the crowds in the temple, the twelve disciples and those to whom he is writing. All would find their faith shaken by the events that lay ahead. Jesus directs them to spiritual resources that will enable them to stand firm.

It is easy to lose ourselves in material like this. The detail is, of course, important, but not at the expense of the broad canvas. This is 'end of the world' stuff, influenced by the prophets and the apocalyptic writers (the best examples in the Bible are Daniel and Revelation). Coming events will bring change, upheaval and distress of earth-shattering importance (signified by the cosmic signs in vv. 11, 25–26). People of faith will be seduced by those who claim to be 'in the know'—false prophets who will gather a following (v. 8). They will be tempted to exchange hope for decadence (vv. 34ff). How, then, can faith withstand the coming deluge?

First, by seeing it as an opportunity to bear testimony (v. 13). As we have seen in Acts, the apostles provide the role models. In all this, trust is vital. Words and wisdom will be given. The power to endure will come from knowing that even in the face of martyrdom, 'not a hair of your head will perish' (v. 18).

Second, by taking the words of Jesus as a trustworthy guide (v. 33). Notice how Luke alters Mark 13:14ff (retained in Matthew 24:15ff), replacing the enigmatic reference to 'the desolating sacrilege' with the more prosaic 'Jerusalem surrounded by armies' (v. 20). He draws on biblical descriptions of the fall of Jerusalem in 587BC (for example, Jeremiah 20:4–5) to make it quite clear to his audience what Jesus had in mind—the destruction of the city in AD70. If Jesus is a reliable guide to the fortunes of Jerusalem, then he can be trusted with the destiny of those who are loyal to him.

Third, by keeping the spiritual senses sharp and alert. Decadence is a form of escapism that dulls the spirit to the true meaning of events.

Hence the need to 'watch at all times' (v. 36). Soon Jesus will give an object lesson in prayerful alertness in the face of screaming distress (22:39ff).

All apocalyptic literature, Jewish as well as Christian, has essentially the same message: 'stand firm in your faith and God will reward you'. The Christian assurance lies in the vindication of Jesus, poetically expressed in the imagery of the coming of the Son of Man (v. 27). God's final victory over the powers of violence will be shared with his saints (see Daniel 7:13–14, 27). The ground of hope lies here.

5 Seeking how to put him to death

Luke 22:1–6, 47–53

Since he arrived in Jerusalem, Jesus has conducted a high-profile public ministry. He claimed the temple as the base for his teaching and, by attracting great crowds, made it impossible for the Jewish leaders to arrest him. How could they achieve their ambitions? Only by separating Jesus from his audience and seizing him with a minimum of fuss. But how?

Insider help, from one of the Twelve, is at hand. Why is Judas willing to betray Jesus into the hands of his enemies? Matthew and John have him driven by greed (Matthew 26:15; John 12:6). Mark and Luke leave the verdict open (Mark 14:10). Some have suggested that Judas was frustrated by Jesus' reticence. He wanted to pressurize him to force the issue of the coming of God's kingdom by bringing him before the Jewish leaders. Whatever was going on in Judas' mind, the leaders are more grateful than any sum of money can say.

When Jesus is finally arrested (vv. 47ff), the benefit of insider knowledge becomes clear. Judas is able to lead a crowd to what is presumably a quiet, secluded place, which Jesus habitually visited. The kiss is an ironic means of identification—a gesture of tenderness that delivers Jesus into violent hands, all the more unnecessary because he is well known to his adversaries. Notice that the disciples are carrying swords. Jesus had apparently encouraged this (see 22:36ff). Their weapons symbolize the way Jesus is now regarded. 'He was reckoned with the transgressors' (22:37, compare Isaiah 53:12;

this is the only quotation from Isaiah 53 in the Gospel passion narratives)—treated as a criminal.

Darkness is the perfect medium for the events now taking shape. What follows is a speedy hearing to confirm the decisions the Jewish leaders have already made; then an attempt to persuade Pilate that he must act swiftly; finally a propaganda coup as a Jew is humiliated at the hands of the Romans. A perfect way to put Jesus to death.

6 I am among you as one who serves

Luke 22:14–27

Leaping ahead in the story allows us to imagine what might have been going on behind the scenes. What about the one who stands centre stage? How would he have us see him? We have wondered what drives Judas. But what motivates Jesus?

He has come to Jerusalem to be acclaimed as its king (19:38). But what kind of king is this, with no army? His only weapons are his words. He has presented himself as a compelling teacher by occupying the seat of learning, the place of wisdom. He has shown himself to be a sharp critic of the holy place and its priests. More than anything, though, he has come to Jerusalem as a pilgrim, to celebrate Passover. He is part of a great movement towards God by those who want to remember the foundations of Israel's existence. More than anything, Jesus is moved by the desire to worship the God of exodus and covenant, who will one day liberate his people when the kingdom of God comes.

Taken up into the memory of his people, Jesus' reading of their history is astute. He knows what is coming to God's beloved son and heir (20:13, 14). Hence his unprecedented actions at the meal table. There is some confusion in the Gospel's textual traditions, as the footnotes show. But there is nothing bewildering in the way bread and cup—so familiar in the Passover liturgy—are invested with new meaning. Whatever his enemies are intent on doing, his life will be given, not taken. His cause will continue in the 'new covenant' sealed by his blood. His followers will gain far more than they lose because his body and blood are given and poured out 'for you'.

The dispute about greatness allows this newly acquired symbolism to speak for itself. As a king and teacher and critic, Jesus reverses conventional ideas about greatness and the use of power, something he has done throughout the Gospel. Here is a Messiah who exercises power for the benefit of others, rather than at their expense. This Son of Man is the faithful Israelite, the man truly devoted to God. He has fused his reading of scripture with the insights that have come to him on the margins of society among tax collectors and sinners. To redeem the world as he knows it will take something other than sectarian holiness or the power of an army. 'This is my body which is given for you... This cup which is poured out for you is the new covenant in my blood... I am among you as one who serves.'

Guidelines

We can see the foundation of Paul's reading of scripture and his understanding of what it means to be Israel in Jesus' debates with the authorities in Jerusalem. Jesus was reluctant to be constrained by particular texts, however venerable, because he realized that their authority came partly from those who interpreted them. What made him disturbing at times was the way he dared to set his own authority as God's son and heir alongside, and sometimes above, all other sources of authority, sacred and secular alike. This makes him no less controversial today.

When the search for authority leads us to insist that 'ours' is the only truth, remind us of Jesus' habitual challenge to all who claim to speak for God in the world.

The vindication of Paul

Paul's journey to Rome begins at last. Though he has escaped from his enemies, he now faces more threats to his life, before taking his gospel to the heart of the empire.

1 They delivered Paul to a centurion

Acts 27:1–12

Paul is in the company of others again. Like Jesus, he is 'reckoned with the transgressors' (compare Luke 22:37)—prisoners who are also to stand trial before the emperor. And there is Aristarchus too, who came with him to Jerusalem (Acts 20:4). The 'we' style of narrative returns here for the first time since 21:18. This may mean that one of Paul's companions is the author of Acts or, at least, the source of material used by the author. Two ships are mentioned. The first (v. 2) travels around the Aegean coast; the second (v. 6) is a grain carrier from Alexandria, taking vital supplies to Rome.

Paul is once more on the receiving end of Gentile kindness. Claudius Lysias, the Roman tribune in Jerusalem, had earlier protected him from the conspiracy of the 'more than forty' (23:12ff). Now the centurion Julius treats him favourably, allowing him leave to make contact with friends in Sidon, who cared for him (v. 3). The contrast between hostility from the Jewish leaders and compassion from their Gentile counterparts is marked.

The journey starts late in the sailing season. 'The fast had already gone by' (v. 9). If this refers to the Day of Atonement, it is already late September or early October. The winds are hardly favourable, and so the second ship sails further south, 'under the lee of Crete', rather than cross the open sea between Greece and Italy.

Paul the experienced traveller speaks in verse 10. From being a silent, passive prisoner, he takes up the role of a prophet, but his voice does not prevail. Julius the centurion is clearly in charge, and follows the majority in the hope that they can reach Phoenix, at the western end of Crete, where they could spend the winter. Paul is under Rome's protection, but it appears that he has merely exchanged one threat for another—the malevolence of the Jewish leaders for the danger of the elements.

We might say that this is Paul's passion journey. Like Jesus on the way to the cross, he is ignored, even rejected. The voyage to Rome is his way of taking up his cross and following Christ daily (Luke 9:23) —the way of the true disciple.

2 There will be no loss of life among you

The gentle south wind that carried the ship along the southern coast of Crete turns into a violent north-easterly gale. This calls for emergency measures—securing the dinghy, running strong ropes under the hull to hold it together, letting down the sea anchor to prevent the ship being driven on to the Syrtis (sandbanks off the coast of north Africa), jettisoning the ship's gear and at least some of the cargo. If the ship were to run aground, it would almost be wrecked.

The sense of despair in verse 20, fed no doubt by exhaustion, is almost tangible. Storm and darkness threaten to return everything to primeval chaos (Genesis 1:2). Little wonder 'all hope of our being saved was at last abandoned'. Paul breaks the silence. He can't resist at least a hint of 'I told you so', but his exhortation is like the creative voice of God speaking into the gloom (Genesis 1:1ff). The words of the angel (this is the only time in Acts that Paul hears the voice of an angel) inspire a confidence rooted in God. Notice how Paul speaks of his faith, describing God as the one 'to whom I belong and whom I worship'. God's promise to Paul of a safe passage extends to his companions on the ship. Paul does not ask them to have faith in God themselves, but to trust his faith. There is a sense in which he believes on their behalf, like those who lowered a paralysed man through the roof of a house in Capernaum, to place him at the feet of Jesus (Luke 5:17ff). Paul's faith is a form of intercession, his promise of salvation like the words of the dying Jesus to the penitent thief (Luke 23:43).

So Paul begins to take charge of the crisis on the ship. His stature grows: no longer ignored and rejected, he is now the prophet of God, speaking words of hope and bringing light into darkness. Chaos is giving birth to salvation.

3 I urge you to take some food

The westward drift towards Malta (Acts 28:1) would take about fourteen days. By now, the crew are intent on saving their own lives.

Rather than go down with the ship, they prepare to launch the dinghy. But they reckon without the alertness of Paul. His concerns are wider. Without skilled sailors, lives could be lost; if the crew remain, there is a greater chance that all 276 (v. 37) on board will survive. The only way to ensure the fulfilment of God's promise is to cut the dinghy's ropes and prevent the crew's escape.

Paul's concerns extend beyond safety to nourishment. Perhaps they have all been without food for fourteen days because they have been fasting and praying. Breaking the fast will encourage them to believe with Paul that disaster has been averted. Notice how he takes the initiative with the bread. He uses a traditional Jewish blessing, with its witness to God as the provider and sustainer of life. Once he has eaten, others follow. We are reminded of other meals in Acts (for example, 2:46; 20:7, 11), and Jesus' feeding of the multitudes (Luke 9:10ff) and the Twelve (Luke 22:14ff).

So there is more to this 'break-fast' than the restoration of bodily strength. Verses 20 and 31 see deliverance from the storm as salvation. The Greek of verse 34 can be translated, 'It will be for your salvation'. Rescue and restoration are instances of the saving power of God, something that the meal on board ship reveals. Other meals have revealed Jesus as servant and redeemer (Luke 22:14ff, 24:28ff). This one presents Paul as a true minister of the crucified and risen Jesus. In his passion, Jesus looks beyond his own interests to the needs of others (the high priest's slave, Luke 22:51; the women of Jerusalem, 23:27ff; the onlookers at his crucifixion, 23:34; the penitent thief, 23:43). Paul does the same. His witness to Jesus comes through deeds rather than words. This is not a time for preaching, but alert and all-embracing service.

4 All escape to land

Acts 27:39—28:10

Once again Paul is on the receiving end of kindness. As the ship, battered by the waves, begins to break up, the soldiers' first thought is to kill their prisoners. But Julius the centurion prevails. Then, on Malta, the locals are kind to the victims of the shipwreck. Later, hospitality is extended to Paul and his companions by Publius, whose father Paul heals. This human benevolence can only reveal the hidden hand of God.

Though safely ashore, Paul exchanges one form of danger for another. The snake drawn out by the heat is, for the superstitious on-lookers, an instrument of divine punishment for a presumed murderer: 'Justice has not allowed him to live' (v. 4). Justice was personified in Greek literature, sometimes as the consort of Zeus. But it turns out that Justice has indeed pronounced her verdict: Paul is innocent, even a god! Luke's audience realize that Paul's rescue derives from the authority given by Jesus to his disciples: 'Behold, I have given you authority to tread on serpents and scorpions' (Luke 10:19). But the verdict of Paul's audience is left unchallenged (unlike the incident in Acts 14:11–18, where Paul berates the people of Lystra who imagine him and Barnabas to be gods). In the eyes of the superstitious Maltese, Paul is innocent before the divine Justice. Again we are reminded of Jesus in his passion, declared righteous (RSV has 'innocent') by the Gentile soldier (Luke 23:47).

Paul the healer recalls Jesus in the Gospel (Luke 4:40; 5:15; 6:18). Like those sent out by Jesus, Paul heals in response to the gift of hospitality (Luke 9:1ff, 10:1ff). So he proves to be a true disciple and apostle. The use of prayer and the laying on of hands is conventional enough, though there is no mention here of the name of Jesus, as elsewhere in Acts (for example, Acts 3:6). As a true minister of Jesus, Paul extends his presence and power without speaking his name.

Luke does not mention any coming to faith on the part of the Maltese, so focused is his narrative on the figure of Paul. Yet Paul here is only an icon of Jesus. Experiencing rejection, interested in more than self-preservation, reaching out to those in need, speaking words of hope and salvation, being declared innocent—Paul is a true disciple and apostle because he is like Jesus, particularly in his passion.

5 And so we came to Rome

Acts 28:11–22

Throughout this final part of the journey, Paul remains in custody (v. 20), though the other prisoners and the soldier guarding him have by now dropped out of the story. Luke gives the impression that progress towards Rome is directed by the 'we' of the narrative—Paul and his companions. Nothing is allowed to deflect our attention from Paul's presence in Rome as the fruit of God's promise.

The theme of brotherhood threads its way through the narrative. The 'Twin Brothers' on the ship (v. 11) are Zeus' twin sons, the patron deities of travellers—though Luke's readers know that Paul's safety comes from 'the God to whom I belong' (27:23). At Puteoli, 'we found brethren' (v. 14), and Paul is in touch with a Christian community once more. Nearing Rome, Paul is met by two groups of 'brethren' (v. 15), 40 miles away at the Forum of Appius and 30 miles out at Three Taverns. Once in Rome, Paul meets more 'brethren', this time the leaders of the dozen or so synagogues serving the Jewish population of about 50,000.

'After three days' (v. 17) may have a ring of Easter about it. It certainly suggests some urgency in Paul's meeting with the Jewish leaders: notice that he takes the initiative in convening them. He introduces himself by declaring his innocence, though in view of the Jews' response in verse 21, this is hardly necessary. It appears that the opposition Paul faced in Jerusalem was orchestrated by a particular group whose interests were hardly representative of Jewish community leaders as a whole. In Rome, Paul is received in a spirit of open-minded enquiry, despite the fact that the movement with which he is associated has attracted a lot of opposition. Paul is keen to make common cause with his audience from the start. He is, first and foremost, a Jew ('our fathers', v. 17; 'my nation', v. 19), whose chief concern is 'the hope of Israel'—the renewal of God's covenant people, and the redemption of the world.

Though Paul has come to Rome to stand before the emperor, we only see him bearing witness to his own people. We are never told what eventually happened to him (Luke's readers would surely have known). What matters is that he has finally arrived in Rome. Just as Jesus travelled to Jerusalem and made it the centre of his movement's mission, so Paul has come to the place from which the gospel can extend 'to the end of the earth' (Acts 1:8). As we shall see, the final scene will leave us in no doubt about the universal scope of the message he has brought to the heart of the empire.

6 He welcomed all who came to him

The final scene is a day of intense discussion and debate. 'The hope of Israel' (28:20) is given another expression familiar to the Jews, 'the kingdom of God', and associated with Jesus, who announced and embodied God's kingdom in his own ministry. 'The kingdom of God and... the Lord Jesus Christ' are the central themes of Paul's teaching in Rome (v. 31).

In all this, Paul sounds the note of continuity. The career of Jesus and his particular understanding of God's kingdom are deeply traditional, rooted in the law of Moses and the prophets. Luke has made this clear throughout his writings. Jesus announced the fulfilment of scripture as he began his ministry in Galilee (Luke 4:16–21). On the Emmaus road he interpreted the meaning of his messianic suffering and glory with the aid of the scriptures (Luke 24:26–27; compare 24:46). And the apostles' testimony in Acts drew on the same scriptures to set out the significance of Jesus' aliveness following his shameful death (for example, Acts 2:30–31). However disturbing or controversial Jesus proved to be among his own people, he stands in the stream of Jewish tradition and culture, flowing from the Bible. Jesus and the scriptures make sense of each other.

Paul also belongs to that same tradition. His message about Jesus and the kingdom receives a mixed response, like the message of Isaiah the prophet before him (vv. 26ff). The verses from the account of the prophet's call in Isaiah 6 are used elsewhere in the New Testament to explain why the gospel sometimes fell on deaf ears (see Luke 8:10; John 12:40; Romans 11:7–8). Given the degree of continuity between Jesus and the Jewish tradition, we might expect a more positive response from his people as a whole. But scripture (in the person of Isaiah) reminds us that we can never take this for granted. Verse 28 should not be understood as suggesting that the Gentiles replace the Jews in God's purposes. Response among them is mixed too, as Luke shows throughout Acts. The point is that Gentiles take their place alongside Jews in the messianic people of God. The apostolic witness started among the Jews as a matter of strategy, but always looked for ways of embracing Gentiles too. Of this, the range of Paul's visitors during his two-year stint in Rome is evidence enough (v. 30).

So Acts ends not with Paul before Caesar or even with his death, but with the apostle as the embodiment of the movement regarded by many as a 'sect' (v. 22). Constantly in dialogue with his Jewish brethren, ever open to Gentiles who are willing to listen to what he has to say about the kingdom of God and the Lord Jesus Christ, Paul—like the one to whom he bears witness—represents a vision of Israel as profoundly Jewish yet extending God's welcome to all.

Guidelines

We have seen two kinds of witness in the final part of the story of Paul. One is in deeds with few words; the other uses words backed up by significant deeds of welcome and hospitality. Words are a necessary part of Christian witness. Among other things, they interpret God's involvement in the world and summon people to participate in this. At the same time, deeds that extend the work of Jesus have their own way of speaking. Words and deeds are both necessary if the Church is to be true to its roots in the ministry of Jesus and the witness of the apostles. Neither is more important than the other; neither is expendable.

Give the Church intelligence and imagination to find words and deeds that convey the grace and challenge of the gospel to those we are called to serve.

The vindication of Jesus

1 Your will… your hour

Luke 22:39–53

The place where Jesus went to pray with his disciples is not named as Gethsemane in this Gospel. All we know is that it was a stone's throw from the Mount of Olives, and somewhere that Jesus often visited. Only here does he tell the disciples to pray, in words that echo the prayer he gave them in 11:4. 'Temptation' is the testing of faith, particularly in the upheaval preceding the coming of God's kingdom. Jesus spoke of this earlier in chapter 21, and at the supper warned Peter in particular of the buffeting that would come his way in what lay ahead (22:31ff). Jesus sees his passion as the prelude to Israel's renewal, and with that the redemption of the world. For this, the Son of Man, and those who follow him to the cross, draw strength through prayer.

In Matthew and Mark, Jesus takes Peter, James and John with him to the place of prayer, as if to support him through his agony. But here he takes steps to be alone. The extent of his anxiety is revealed in verses 43 and 44, which are missing from some of the earliest Gospel manuscripts. As the disciples' grief submerges them in sleep, so Jesus' agony drives him to prayer. His petition is nothing if not honest. 'Father, if thou art willing, remove this cup from me' pleads for some other way to fulfil God's will. But far more important than avoiding the violence he has long anticipated (9:22ff) is Jesus' readiness to set his own fears aside: 'Nevertheless not my will, but thine, be done.' Here and in the upper room, Jesus lives what he taught his followers to pray. Today he has given his disciples the bread of his own body and spoken of the coming of God's kingdom. Now he asks for the strength to do God's will, as faith is put to the severest test.

Judas is not among the sleeping disciples. We can imagine him slipping away while Jesus and the others walk to the Mount of Olives, to give his paymasters the tip-off. There is a curious mixture of tenderness and violence as Jesus is arrested. The would-be kiss, the injury to the high priest's slave—and Jesus at the heart of it all, stretching out his hand to heal as if nothing in the world were more important. He meets the Jewish leaders with incredulity rather than resistance. Why come after him armed? Why now, rather than earlier in the temple? The night-time arrest symbolizes the passing of control over events from Jesus to his enemies. 'This is your hour, and the power of darkness' (v. 53). But only for so long: 'thy will be done'.

2 Are you the King of the Jews?

Luke 22:66—23:16

Once he is arrested, Jesus really is on his own. The disciples are not rounded up: however much of a threat Jesus presents to the authorities, there is nothing to warrant taking his followers too. Peter comes closest to sticking by him, but he falters badly in the high priest's courtyard (22:54–62). The prisoner is forced to endure the customary humiliation rituals, and appears before the ruling council early the next day. We should not think of Jesus facing a formal trial. The authorities have already made up their minds about him. All they need is a pretext to deliver him to the Roman governor as deserving death.

Their initial enquiry seeks to establish whether Jesus thinks of himself as Messiah. His replies are both elusive and allusive. 'Son of man' alludes to Daniel's vision of the vindication of God's faithful ones, who receive the kingdom and reign for ever (Daniel 7:13, 14, 27). Jesus may have passed into the hands of his enemies, but God will see to it that he and his cause triumph over the powers of darkness: 'thy will be done'. 'Are you the Christ... the Son of God?' No straight answers, but enough for the authorities to deliver him to Pilate as 'Christ, a king' (v. 2).

This account of Jesus' appearance before the Roman governor is fuller than the one in Matthew and Mark. 'Perverting our nation, and forbidding us to give tribute to Caesar' suggests that Jesus is accused of seducing the Jews away from their loyalty to Rome. How hypocritical! We recall that he hardly spoke unequivocally against paying Roman taxes (20:22ff), but there was evidently enough imprecision to allow his enemies to twist his words. Pilate is in Jerusalem to make sure that order is maintained in a city overflowing with pilgrims. He is not the weak figure we often think he is. Sources outside the Gospels describe him as ruthless, with a cruel streak. He finds Jesus innocent, even when the Jewish authorities insist that he is a troublemaker. But Pilate is not really interested in him, and welcomes the chance to pass him on to Herod Antipas, ruler of Galilee, also in town for the Passover.

Only in Luke are we told of Jesus' meeting with Herod. We can imagine the scene—Jesus facing screaming accusations, cynical mockery and ritual humiliation. Still he remains silent. Who *really* has the upper hand? For all his powerlessness, for all that he is passed from one ruler to another, Jesus manages to bring enemies together. The Gentile governor and the Jewish king 'became friends with one another that very day' (v. 12). Jesus' true messianic power—the power of reconciliation—is undiminished, even on the way to the cross.

3 Delivered up to their will

Luke 23:13–25

Herod's lengthy interrogations don't advance the Jewish leaders' cause. The best Pilate can offer them is punishment prior to release. Not surprisingly, this is unacceptable to those who have gone to a lot of trouble to arrest Jesus. They are not going to let him slip through their fingers just because Pilate and Herod can't see how dangerous he is. By this time, the Jewish authorities have been joined by another group—'the people' (v. 13). Presumably they are locals, inhabitants of the city who are easily persuaded to bay for Jesus' blood—and with good reason. The chief priests will have pointed out that Jesus' words and actions against the temple could have disastrous consequences for the economy of Jerusalem. The locals have a lot to lose if Jesus and his cause are allowed to flourish. There is only one way to prevent this: 'Crucify him.'

There is no evidence outside the Gospels for the custom of releasing a prisoner at Passover-tide, though in view of what lay at the heart of the festival—the celebration of the release of the Hebrew slaves from Egypt—it would be a fitting symbol. Barabbas (the name means 'son of the father') is a terrorist. Is he perhaps a local man? He is certainly more popular among these crowds than Jesus. Does Pilate cynically manipulate his audience? He does not care either way whether Jesus or Barabbas lives or dies. But this is his chance, when the Jews are celebrating freedom, to remind them that they are still in captivity to a foreign power. Executing Jesus or Barabbas will make the same point: Rome rules. Shame one Jew, shame them all. So Pilate takes the line of least resistance. Perhaps the noisy crowd makes him think that their leaders have a point. Jesus disturbs the peace enough to warrant official action against him. Crucifying Jesus will keep the chief priests happy, the mob quiet, Jerusalem calm and its pilgrims mindful of the sovereign power of the emperor.

Pilate '*delivered* Jesus up to their will' (v. 25), just as Judas 'betrayed him to [the Jewish authorities]' (22:6). The verb is the same in Greek. So the work of Judas is complete. In one sense, the same is true of Jesus. Throughout his ordeal, he does not raise his voice. His silence is eloquent testimony to the hidden power of God. Jesus is bold enough to believe that the last word lies not with the mob or the Jewish authorities or Pilate, but the Father in whose name he acts and whose will he fulfils by giving his body and pouring out his blood. His silence discloses his strength.

4 Save yourself!

Luke 23:32–43

A Jewish festival was an ideal time for a public execution. What better way to ensure its maximum propaganda impact? Luke alone omits the name 'Golgotha'. The place where Jesus and the others are crucified is simply called 'Skull', perhaps because executions regularly happened there, or because the place was shaped like a skull. The inscription bearing the charge has Jesus crucified as a would-be Messiah. The narrative is sparse, as in the other Gospels. The evangelists could presume that their audiences knew what happened at a crucifixion. The absence of detail allows them to focus on what they see as the meaning of it all, which comes out in the words from the cross and the events taking shape as Jesus is executed.

Jesus' words differ from one Gospel to another. 'Father, forgive them' (v. 34) is missing from some manuscripts, but it is typical of Jesus' concern for others. Even as he dies, his ability to reach out is undiminished. The Son of Man provides the pattern for his followers: Stephen, the first martyr, also asked God to forgive those who murdered him (Acts 7:60). Dividing up the victims' clothes was common enough, like sharing out the spoils of battle. Alert readers will spot the allusion to Psalm 22:18, with its description of the fate of the righteous sufferer. The spectators here stand in silence, unlike those in Matthew and Mark. Only the Jewish leaders and the Roman soldiers mock, exploiting the irony of a so-called Messiah now stripped of clothes, followers and reputation. Soon his life too will expire. 'He saved others; let him save himself' (v. 35). But this Son of Man Messiah saves his life by losing it in the cause of God's kingdom (9:23ff). Only by giving himself away will he renew God's covenant people and redeem the world (22:20).

The scene in verses 39–43 is found only in Luke, and harks back to 22:37. The first criminal is right: according to popular expectation, this is no way for the Messiah to do his work. But the second is more perceptive. They are only getting what they deserve, but not so Jesus (another declaration of his innocence). The so-called 'penitent thief' sees that Jesus really is the Christ. This is no mockery of the saving power of God, but its truest revelation. Only through crucifixion does the Son of Man Messiah come into his kingdom. This criminal wants to be included when the saints of the Most High inherit God's everlasting rule (Daniel 7:27). And again Jesus finds the strength to reach out.

'Paradise' is a Persian word meaning 'park' or 'garden'. Contemporary (non-biblical) Jewish texts used it as an image of God's coming kingdom. The end will be like the beginning: Paradise is Eden restored. 'Today you will be with me in Paradise': the penitent, perceptive criminal will share in the fruits of Jesus' sacrifice, without delay.

5 Certainly this man was innocent

Luke 23:44–49

The meaning of Jesus' crucifixion is also brought out by the circumstances surrounding it. Darkness has long been a symbol of divine judgment (see Amos 8:9ff). Here it is caused by an eclipse, which in the ancient world was a sign of doom, as if the sun were turning away from what was happening. Jesus had earlier spoken of 'signs in the sun and moon and stars' that would signal the end of the present, unredeemed world order and herald the coming of God's kingdom (see 21:25f). So the crucifixion marks the turning point, as one era gives way to another.

Luke places the tearing of the temple curtain before Jesus' death (v. 45); in Mark it comes afterwards, at the climax of the narrative. Here its symbolic significance is reduced. Though Jesus has announced the end of the temple, it continues to play a key part in the life of the church in Jerusalem, as we have seen. But it does not occupy the place in the new order that it had in the old, as the symbolic centre of God's covenant people. There is no cry of desolation ('My God, my God, why have you forsaken me?'), as there is in Mark and Matthew. Jesus' last words are taken from the prayer of another righteous sufferer (Psalm 31:5), on whom 'the scorn of all my adversaries' has fallen. However drained and humiliated he may be, nothing can diminish Jesus' faith in his heavenly 'Father'.

The responses of those who are close enough to see Jesus die could not be more different. The spectators beat their breasts in shame; the centurion is so moved that he praises God. 'Certainly this man was innocent' echoes the verdicts of Pilate, Herod and one of the criminals. But the Greek word *dikaios* means 'righteous', not just innocent, as in Psalm 31:18. The way Jesus dies shows that he is worthy of God's blessing and honour. And he dies as he has lived, utterly loyal to God and his cause. His faith is such that he can expect God to vindicate him, despite the judgments of those who have crucified him.

There is a strong Jewish tradition of suffering righteous figures who can expect to be vindicated. We find them in the Psalms (for example, 22; 35), Isaiah 53 (the servant), Wisdom 2 (the son of God) and Daniel 7 (the saints of the Most High, represented by the one like a son of man). Jesus gathers up these hopes and transforms them, through the vindication we know as 'the resurrection of the dead'. The Gentile centurion acknowledges the faith *of* Jesus, and paves the way for faith *in* Jesus. 'Certainly this man is righteous'—and is later declared to be the Righteous One (Acts 3:14; 7:52).

6 In a rock-hewn tomb, where no one had been laid

Luke 23:50–56

Not all members of the Jewish ruling council, the Sanhedrin, behaved reprehensibly towards Jesus. Joseph of Arimathea is a dissenting voice. As one who is 'looking for the kingdom of God', he is probably a Pharisee. So he would be concerned about matters of purity. To leave Jesus hanging on the cross would only bring further shame on the land (Deuteronomy 21:23). Hence Joseph's desire to give Jesus a decent burial. A 'rock-hewn tomb' was the preserve of the wealthy; the poor were buried in the ground, and criminals were thrown into a common grave. Jesus is wrapped and laid in a new tomb, honoured far more in his burial than in his death.

The Galilean women were standing at a distance from the Skull. Shock and grief would not allow them to come any closer. But they were near enough to see what happened to the body of Jesus. It is not clear why Joseph does not anoint Jesus' body when he buries him. So there is work for the women to do, but not yet. The sabbath is about to start. Luke is careful to point out that everything happens in accordance with the law.

After the way Jesus has been treated in the last hours of his life—mockery, humiliation, cruelty, violence—it comes as a relief that his dead body is treated with the respect due to a righteous man. On Holy Saturday, it is good to allow our thoughts and feelings to come to rest on Joseph's honouring of Jesus, as a way of preparing ourselves for all that we will celebrate tomorrow.

Guidelines

A meditation for Easter Day, based on Luke 24:1–35

Where does Easter faith begin?

With the soldier on duty
we praise God for what we have seen
of undying faith and boundless compassion.
But this is not enough.

With Joseph of Arimathea
we honour the bruised and broken body
of one who is worthy of the greatest respect.
But again, this is not enough.

With the women, and Peter and the other disciples,
we make our way to the tomb and find the body gone.
But the words of the angels do not bring us to faith.
Even they are not enough.

With Cleopas and his companion we walk home to Emmaus,
and a stranger comes to join us.
We hear them tell him what happened to their friend
and how this has shattered all their dreams.
We listen as the stranger breaks open the scriptures
and weaves a pattern of suffering and glory
that excites us with the hope of liberation.
But still this is not enough.

We sit at table and watch the stranger
as he breaks and blesses and gives out the bread.
Something stirs in the memory.
Only one says grace like this and he is dead.
Before we have time to find out his name
he is gone.

An empty tomb might mean many things,
but today only this:
The crucified one is truly alive,
his shame turned into his greatest honour.
He who saved others by losing himself
is known in the breaking of scriptures and bread.
The Lord has risen indeed,
and we are drawn into something that feels like humanity's springtime.

FURTHER READING

C.F. Evans, *Saint Luke* (SCM Press, 1990), contains a wealth of detail on the Gospel

James D.G. Dunn, *The Acts of the Apostles* (Epworth Press, 1996), is an accessible commentary that does not shirk the historical problems raised by Luke's writings

Charles H. Talbert, *Reading Luke* (Crossroad, 1989), and F. Scott Spencer, *Acts* (Sheffield Academic Press, 1997), take a literary approach to the Gospel and Acts

John Bowker (ed.), *The Complete Bible Handbook* (Dorling Kindersley, 1998), includes a number of brief and beautifully illustrated articles on issues related to Luke's writings

ISAIAH 40—55:
A VISION OF HOPE FOR EXILES

There is something about Isaiah 40—55 that marks it out from the rest of the book of Isaiah. Even at first glance, it is easy to see that something changes between the end of chapter 39 and the beginning of chapter 40. The first 39 chapters of the book of Isaiah speak, with only a few exceptions, of the coming destruction of Judah. Isaiah's message here is of devastation and doom. In chapter 40, the mood changes entirely: the next sixteen chapters promise consolation in place of devastation, hope in place of despair.

This apparent change of mood seems to indicate a new context for the prophetic message. The early chapters of Isaiah seem to be set between about 750 and 700BC, as the reigns of four kings, Uzziah, Jotham, Ahaz and Hezekiah, are all mentioned. Isaiah 40—55, by contrast, has a different backdrop. These chapters seem to look forward to the end of the exile and a return from Babylon to Judah. In particular, King Cyrus of Persia (45:1ff.) is heralded as God's agent in bringing about a significant change of fortune for the people of God, which sets the background for this part of Isaiah in the late sixth century BC, with the hope of rescue and restoration for the exiled people of God. The dating of this section indicates that it is unlikely that the author is Isaiah of Jerusalem, but the person or people who wrote it remain anonymous throughout. For the sake of ease, therefore, we shall use the name Isaiah when referring to the author(s) of this part of the book.

The great theme of these chapters is God's dramatic intervention in the fate of the exiles—an intervention which, unlike the terrible events leading up to the exile, will be one of comfort. The prophet's hope here can be described as eschatological. The word literally means a study of the end times. It has popularly become associated with catastrophes of immense proportion but it is more properly associated with God's dramatic intervention in the world at some point in the future. This intervention is sometimes expected to herald salvation and vindication, though at other times it promises suffering and punishment. Isaiah's prophecies of hope and restoration present to us the side of eschatology which is characterized by redemption. Isaiah presents here a vision of a world redeemed by God.

The Easter season highlights a similar theme and so makes it highly appropriate to study this section of Isaiah at Easter. The themes of new life, new birth and new hope that arise in both Isaiah 40—55 and the Easter message illuminate our understanding of a God who yearns to redeem and restore the world.

The NRSV has been used throughout.

1 Comfort my people

Isaiah 40:1–2

Isaiah's message of hope for the people in exile begins with comfort. God's first action in rebuilding and restoring a lost and devastated people is to bring them comfort in their suffering. Isaiah recognizes that before the people can begin even to prepare for God's dramatic action in the world, they need to be reassured and consoled.

The new beginning marked by this chapter commences with a request for someone to bring this message of consolation to the people of God. One of the features of this passage, which cannot be conveyed by our English translations, is that this request is addressed not to one person but to many people—the command is a plural one. God calls here for someone to hear his message of comfort and to relay it to his people. This has a similar effect to that of God's call of Isaiah in 6:8, where he asks, 'Whom shall I send?' The difference here lies in the content of the message. In Isaiah 6 the prophet is charged to announce a message of devastation and gloom; here the message is of comfort and hope.

The task that God sets for anyone who will hear it is that they are to speak to the heart of God's people and reassure them that their punishment is over. The anger that brought about the suffering and pain for God's people has now passed and a glorious future lies ahead.

The message of comfort that God proclaims comes to the people like sunshine after rain, and with it comes a promise not just of a cessation of the bad times but of the glorious future that lies ahead. In a similar way, Jesus' resurrection on Easter day brought solace to those who grieved for Jesus' death but also a glorious hope of things to come. This double strand of ending and new beginning is the essence of eschatology. Although we often talk about eschatology as the ultimate ending, it is really the ultimate new beginning, and this lies at the heart of Isaiah's message here.

2 In the wilderness prepare the way

Isaiah 40:3–5

The opening chapters of Isaiah 40—55 contain various different voices crying out their message. We began in verses 1–2 with the voice of God calling for a messenger to carry a message of consolation to the people. The next voice we hear is a single disembodied voice—whose identity we never discover—picking up the cry. This voice acts as a herald going before the Lord to make preparations.

We have become so familiar with this passage—picked up, as it is, in the Gospel accounts in relation to John the Baptist—that the incongruity of it has become lost. This disembodied voice commands that a large road be built for God through the most inhospitable of desert places. The image of filling up valleys and levelling mountains is reminiscent of 21st-century motorway construction. The purpose of this highway is to make a way for God to return to his people. The prophet Ezekiel movingly described God's abandonment of the temple and also of the people immediately before the temple's destruction in 586BC (Ezekiel 11:22–23). This passage provides the other side of the story: the preparation for God's return. The disembodied, anonymous voice cries out that the time has come to prepare the earth for God's return.

One question that arises in relation to this passage is about where the voice is when it is crying out this message. The Greek translators of the Hebrew Bible assumed that the voice was crying out in the wilderness (v. 3, 'A voice cries out in the wilderness: "Prepare the way…'), and this tradition was picked up by the Gospel writers (for example, in Mark 1:3). In fact, in the Hebrew text, it is not the voice that is in the wilderness but the preparation for God's return ('A voice cries out: "In the wilderness prepare the way…"'). This is important. It is the labouring in the wilderness, in the barren and inhospitable places, that makes true preparation for God's return. Those prepared to labour in the desert places are promised a vision of God's glory.

3 See, the Lord God comes

Isaiah 40:6–11

In verse 6, our series of voices continues with a conversation. A voice (it is not clear whether it is the same one as before or a different one) says, 'Cry out!' and 'I' (presumably the prophet) say, 'What shall I cry?' Through this exchange, we begin to see that the action of the prophet is not isolated. It joins in with a process that has begun before the time of this passage and continues afterwards. The prophet's role is a vital one but not the only one in God's plan. The prophet is simply joining in with a process already begun by God.

The first part of the message that God gives to the prophet is of his constancy. God is not to be compared with the passing, temporary things of the earth. In a transient world, words are perhaps the most transient of all—uttered one minute and gone the next. In contrast, God's word stands for ever. Even the most temporary of things associated with God will last for ever.

From here, Isaiah addresses Zion/Jerusalem (v. 9: these two words mean the same thing—Mount Zion is often used in the Bible as another word for Jerusalem). Isaiah's message to Jerusalem is that she is to declare the good news of God's arrival to the cities of Judah (v. 10, 'See, the Lord God comes with might'). The chain of God's message continues—from a call to anyone who will listen in verse 1 to a single voice that takes up the cry (vv. 3, 6), to the prophet (v. 6) and now to the very recipients of God's message (v. 9). Jerusalem is drawn into the message of hope and salvation. Only when she takes up the cry herself can she recognize the message of comfort that God proclaims. Jerusalem's message to the other cities of Judah is that the

God who comes with might (v. 10) is also a shepherd who feeds his flock and gathers his lambs (v. 11). It is Jerusalem's recognition of the true nature of God, and her willingness to proclaim it, which in the end brings comfort to God's people.

4 Rising with wings like eagles

Isaiah 40:27–31

Despite the glorious vision in 40:11, which envisages Jerusalem announcing God's message of comfort, the announcement does not take place immediately. Although we do not know exactly what Jacob/Israel (again, two words that mean the same thing) has said, the gist of their complaint is clear. The people seem convinced that God is unwilling to help them, claiming that their 'way is hidden from the Lord' and their 'right is disregarded' (v. 27). The people feel that God has turned away from them.

In response, the prophet makes four affirmations about the nature of God (v. 28). The first pair of affirmations describes two basic characteristics of God: he is everlasting and he is the creator of the ends of the earth. These two attributes are ascribed to God over and over again in this part of Isaiah. The second pair of affirmations continue from the first pair: such a God does not faint or grow weary, and his understanding is unsearchable. Because of this, the human mind cannot comprehend when or how God will act, but the people can be assured that when God does act, it will be to offer them a share of God's own strength. Those who wait for the moment of God's intervention in the world will find their feeble humanity transformed by the strength and vitality of God. They, like eagles, will soar above the earth on wings that apparently never tire.

Isaiah's response to the complaint of God's people is to reaffirm who God is (he is everlasting and the creator) and to point out that human beings cannot hope to understand God. At the same time, he offers the promise of transformation to those who are prepared to wait for him to act. Isaiah puts his finger here on a classic human complaint—that God does not act when we want him to. When we experience this, it is tempting to assume that God is unwilling to act or does not care, but this is untrue. God will act when the time is right, but the challenge to our feeble, weary human selves is to hang on and wait for that time. If we do, Isaiah assures us, the reward will be great.

5 I am the first and the last

Isaiah 41:1–5

The previous passage contained the prophet's defence of God in the face of Israel's complaint. Here God defends himself. It is a characteristic of Isaiah's writing in this part of the book to portray mock trial scenes in which God defends himself. The image used is of a civil action in which there are two plaintiffs, one who brings the action and the other who defends himself or herself. A third party is called upon to decide whether or not the action is to be upheld.

The complainant here is Israel, who is complaining, as we discovered above, that God is unwilling to help. The defendant is God and the adjudicators, somewhat surprisingly, are Israel's near neighbours. The coastlands are the countries along the Mediterranean coast. The idea is that God is so clearly in the right that even Israel's historic enemies will be able to see it.

God's defence is conducted on a different level from Isaiah's. Isaiah used the nature of God to argue against the Israelite complaint; God uses something even more concrete. It is untrue, says the defence, that God is unwilling to act—he has begun to do so already. The victor from the east (v. 2) is Cyrus, king of Persia, who was sweeping through the lands of the ancient Near East, conquering all in his path. Although the exiles are still in captivity in Babylon, God has begun a chain of events which will lead to their eventual release and return home. What is most striking of all, here, is that God will stop at nothing to redeem his people. He will even create a new world empire to achieve his ends because he is, as we have learnt already, everlasting —he is first and will be with the last (v. 4), or, as Revelation 1:8 puts it, he is the alpha and the omega.

6 You are my servant

Isaiah 41:8–10

God's defence of himself, begun in 41:1–5, continues here as God addresses Israel. God's words to the people of Israel confirm that they are important in his plan for the world. Israel is 'his servant' and chosen especially by God (vv. 8–9). As the offspring of Abraham, God's friend, Israel is to be assured of God's continued care and concern.

The election of Israel as God's chosen people is shown to be a gathering of the people from the ends of the earth. Not only did God choose Israel to be his people, he also gathered them from the four corners of the earth. The text does not make it clear when this gathering took place and perhaps this is deliberate. The mention of Abraham brings to mind the calling of Abraham from Mesopotamia to Canaan. In a sense, he was gathered from Ur (which, during the exilic period, became Babylon) to Canaan (which became Israel). The reference might also bring to mind the calling of Israel out of Egypt at the exodus, to a new home in the promised land. The ambiguity of the phrasing serves to emphasize the idea that election involves not just a choosing but also a gathering. The fear of the exiles that their dispersion in Babylon would lead to God abandoning them is unfounded. Just as God has called and gathered them in the past, so he will do it again.

God goes on to comfort the people with promises of a present reality as well as a future hope. They are not to fear, because their God is with them ('for I am with you… for I am your God') and he will strengthen them, help them and uphold them (v. 10). God has called and gathered them in the past, is with them in the present, and will also strengthen and encourage them in the future.

Guidelines

God yearns to redeem and restore his people. The passages that we have explored this week have stressed this fact over and over again. In the writings of Isaiah, we encounter a God who will stop at nothing to draw his people into relationship with himself. This same God was even prepared, 500 years after Isaiah, to send his Son into the world to die and rise again. This was an entirely new action by God but it comes as no surprise to those who have read Isaiah. This kind of God is exactly the kind of God who might go so far in his concern for his people as to send his only Son into the world.

What is surprising, though, is that God seeks our help. God cries out in 40:1 for someone to comfort his people. Today, God still waits, yearning for us to pick up his cry of comfort to the world. And how desperately our world needs to hear this message—a message that proclaims, in the constantly shifting and changing world in which we live, that God and his word remain for ever.

God calls—but will you answer?

19–25 April

1 Here is my servant

Isaiah 42:1–4

In this passage, God presents to us his servant—a servant who will bring about God's rule of justice on the earth (v. 4b). The servant will achieve this mammoth task through the most surprising of means— he or she will be quiet, gentle and caring. The servant will not destroy even the most hopeless of causes but will nourish the world quietly and gently until even those who have never recognized God in the past wait with eager anticipation for his teaching (v. 4c).

Of course, especially at this time of the year, we cannot help but see the figure of Christ in this prophecy. Who else established so much justice on the earth? Who else's teaching caused so many to wait for more? Who else was so gentle and so quiet in achieving so much? Jesus fulfilled these expectations perfectly.

Yet we have to ask whether he was the only person that Isaiah had in mind here. Jesus fulfilled this prophecy better than anyone else before or since, but that does not necessarily limit the role to him alone. This passage is often considered as part of the 'servant songs' (the others are 49:1–6; 50:4–9 and 52:13—53:12). All of these songs seem to refer in a personal way to a particular servant figure. This has caused many people to spend a considerable amount of time attempting to work out who it is. Is it one person or Israel as a nation? Is it the prophet himself or the king? Is it a real person or an ideal type? The questions roll on and so do the answers, but behind all the complexity lies a simple response. This servant does the work of God in the world, as God would have it done. It is not surprising, therefore, that Christ fulfils the prophecy so well—only he managed to carry out God's work in the world so perfectly.

Perhaps, therefore, the servant portrayed here is not so much a real person as a job description. God's servants throughout the centuries have all fitted this description—though none as perfectly as Christ himself. This passage may be God's advertisement for all those who would be his servants in the world—all may apply, and no previous experience is necessary.

2 A light to the nations

Isaiah 42:5–9

In this passage, God continues to speak, but now addresses someone directly (v. 6) and commissions them for their task in the world (vv. 6–7). The identity of the person whom God is addressing is unclear. It may be the servant of 42:1–4 or someone else. In a sense, the identity of the person addressed is unimportant because the task assigned to them is the task assigned to us all.

The charge given in verse 7 will sound familiar to readers of the Gospels because it is like the passage that Jesus read out in the synagogue at the start of his ministry: 'The Spirit of the Lord is upon me, because he has anointed me to bring good news to the poor. He has sent me to proclaim release to the captives and recovery of sight to the blind…' (Luke 4:18, quoting Isaiah 61:1). Jesus chose to use a passage very similar to 42:5–9 to identify his own ministry in the world. This commission, therefore, is as valid in the new covenant as in the old. We, like Jesus, are charged to bring light where there is darkness, sight where there is blindness and freedom where there is oppression.

As well as laying out this commission, God also gives a reason for it, and the reason is twofold—the nature of God (v. 5) and of our relationship with him (v. 6). God is the creator of the whole world and each individual within it. The words used of God's creative act depict care and nurture both on a grand scale and on a detailed scale. God stretches out the heavens and gives breath to the tiniest baby; God spreads out the earth and gives the breath of life to those who walk on it. Whether it be the greatest or the smallest thing in creation, God is a God who cares for and nurtures it.

At the same time as creating us, God calls us into relationship with himself. He calls us, takes us by our hand and then gives us as a covenant to the nations. We usually understand a commission as something given to us. Here the opposite takes place—we are given to the world: 'I have given you as a covenant to the nations...' (v. 6). Being in relationship with God demands that we look outward to those around, seeking to be the gift to the world that God has called us to be.

3 Like a woman in labour

Isaiah 42:14–16

It comes as something of a surprise to find God described here as like a woman about to give birth. We do not often think of God as having extreme emotions but here the most extreme of all feelings is attributed to him. The image is a powerful one. At the start of labour, it is possible to keep still, to be restrained and make no noise (v. 14), but as labour continues, it becomes increasingly impossible to be still and the cries made become louder and louder. At the same time, the person in labour will often feel overwhelmingly angry and strong, so the description of devastation and drought in verse 15 fits well: many women in labour feel like doing such things!

The whole purpose of labour, however, is to give birth, and strong emotions during labour give way quickly to tenderness. Exactly the same happens here. The devastation to be wreaked, presumably on Judah's captors, is followed swiftly by a description of compassion for God's own people. God will bring the people out of exile, back home.

On the way home, they will encounter new experiences but are to feel assured that God is leading them all the way (v. 16). This experience of encountering new things before we get to a place that feels like 'home' will be familiar to many people. Indeed, often it is only through the experience of encountering unknown paths that we can begin to trust that it is God himself who leads us home.

The people of God are described here, as they often are in Isaiah, as 'the blind', because they cannot or will not see the plans that God has for them. It is interesting to notice that God's promise is not to open their eyes immediately, but to lead them to safety and only later to 'turn the darkness before them into light' (v. 16). In their blindness, the people are called upon to put their trust in God—and when they do so, perhaps they will discover that they are not so blind after all.

4 Do not fear

Isaiah 43:1–7

This passage begins with a profound message of reassurance. The people are not to fear, because the God who created them has called them to be his own and has redeemed them (v. 1). The language that Isaiah uses here to describe the relationship between God and his people is significant. God has formed not only the bodies of the chosen people but also the nation. The people were formed as God's own people through the exodus, the greatest act of redemption so far in their history. Thus we see a God who created the world and continues to create it and recreate it in his acts of redemption. In this short verse (v. 1) we get an important insight into God's action in the world. God created the world at the dawn of time but has continued to create and recreate it throughout history. Confidence in God and lack of fear can be based on God's repeated intervention in the lives of his people. How can the exiles be sure that God will act to save them? Because he has done so again and again in the past. How do we know that God will help us? Because God has intervened in the lives of his people so often before, and part of the point of reading the Bible is to remind us of this.

The God who has acted in this way throughout history vows to act again to save his people. Even in situations of the most extreme danger—in water and fire—the people of God can be certain that God is with them. It is important to recognize, however, that God does not promise that the people will not experience danger. God's promise is simply that he will be with them as they walk 'through the waters' and 'through fire' (v. 2) so that they are not overwhelmed or consumed. God's care does not promise freedom from things that frighten us but the ability to cope with them.

The ultimate goal of God's promise here is to gather back together again 'everyone who is called by my name' (v. 7). Just as he formed Israel in the first place, God's concern is to recreate Israel from the lost and scattered exiles. Wherever they are in the world, God will gather his people back together again, because they are precious in his sight and he loves them (v. 4).

5 I am about to do a new thing

Isaiah 43:16–21

Isaiah once more picks up the theme of the exodus but this time the reference is much more obvious. The God who can part the seas and defeat a mighty army is the God who now speaks to the people in exile. The implication of the statement is that, if God can do such a mighty act in the face of the Egyptian army, the Babylonian empire can also be defeated. The people should not for one minute imagine that this God could not save them from their captors.

Having established this, however, Isaiah's message takes on a new twist. The God of the exiles is the same God who has performed these wondrous acts in the past, but this is not what they are to concentrate on. The exiles are not to remember 'the former things' or the things 'of old' (v. 18) but to look forward to the new things that God is about to do among them (v. 19). It can be easy to spend so long remembering the glorious things that God has done in the past that we forget to look forward to the glorious events of the future. Concentration on the events of the exodus could detract the exiles from fully expecting God's glorious intervention in their own lives.

The new thing that God is about to do is revolutionary: he is about to transform the desert from a barren, dangerous wilderness into a safe, peaceful oasis. The wilderness will have water flowing through it and the wild animals will be so busy worshipping God that they will not attack the people who pass by. This indeed is a new thing. In the exodus, the people of God spent 40 years wandering in the barren, dangerous wilderness until they were allowed to enter the promised land. The problem for the exiles is that the events of the exile turned their land flowing with milk and honey into a desolate place. Isaiah tells us earlier in the book that the land will become a wasteland (for example, 6:11: 'Until cities lie waste without inhabitant, and houses without people, and the land is utterly desolate'). Here God transforms the land from desolation to comfort, from wilderness to oasis. The God we worship is the God who can transform even the most barren of desert places—our challenge is to perceive it.

6 The Lord's anointed

Isaiah 45:1–7

This passage is one of the most startling in the whole of Isaiah. In it, Isaiah speaks of the Lord's anointed one or Messiah. At this point, the word Messiah had not gained the connotations that it had during the time of Jesus but was used of people within Israel chosen to perform a particular task. The word is used in connection with prophets and priests in the Old Testament but is most commonly used to refer to kings. It would therefore come as something of a shock to hear Isaiah talk of a foreign king as being the Lord's anointed. The exiles have to come to terms with the knowledge that God will use the most unexpected, even shocking, person to fulfil his plan for them.

The connection between God and Cyrus goes even further than God marking Cyrus out as 'his anointed' (v. 1). God also called Cyrus by name and gave him an honorific title ('surname' in the NRSV, v. 4). Isaiah makes it clear that God knows Cyrus, even if Cyrus does not know God (v. 4). Cyrus' lack of recognition or understanding of God does nothing to hinder God's plan for the world. It is awe-inspiring, and a little humbling, to discover that although God invites humanity to join in with his plan for the world, they do not need to do so for this plan to be fulfilled. God's concern for his chosen people is so great that he does not wait for Cyrus to accept him before he acts.

As a Persian, Cyrus worshipped many gods, including the Babylonian god Marduk, but never, as far as we know, Yahweh. The futility of such worship is something that Isaiah draws out in this passage. The prophet is uncompromising: there are no other gods beside Yahweh, he is the only one and Cyrus serves him whether he knows it or not. God has created everything in the world and everything can be traced back to him. This leads us to encounter something rather uncomfortable: if God has created everything, he has created both good and bad things ('I make weal and create woe', v. 7). This is both inspiring and troubling. It is good to live in a world governed entirely by God but disturbing to be told that God created evil as well as good. This God whom we worship is awesome and powerful but leaves us with profound questions with which we must wrestle.

Guidelines

This week we have encountered some of the many facets of God's nature. We have seen a God who cares for his people, who created the whole world and everything in it, who has redeemed his people and continues to do so, and the God who 'makes weal and creates woe' (45:7). We must remind ourselves that the God who now wants to call his people back to himself sent them into exile in the first place. As Christians, we struggle with this view of God—with a God responsible for suffering as well as for healing.

It is tempting to say that this God of the Old Testament is not the God that we worship today. To a certain extent this is true, but if we rush too quickly to this conclusion we bypass something important. The problem of suffering is one to which we can give no easy answers, and passages such as these in Isaiah remind us that we should not try to. The God whom we worship is much bigger than our human understanding. When God appeared to Job out of the whirlwind, Job was forced to say, 'I have uttered what I did not understand, things too wonderful for me, which I did not know' (Job 42:3). God is too great for our human minds to grasp and yet this God is prepared to stoop down to each one of us to say, 'Do not fear, for I have redeemed you... When you pass through the waters, I will be with you' (Isaiah 43:1–2).

1 Before I was born

Isaiah 49:1–6

Isaiah 42:1–4 is regarded as being the first of four servant songs in Isaiah; this passage is considered to be the second. Yet, on an initial reading, this passage looks as though it should come first. It seems to be talking about the call of the servant which, as in Jeremiah 1:5, occurred while the servant was still in the womb. Even then, we are told, God gave the servant the attributes that he would need for later ministry (v. 2).

There is a problem, however, with this passage, which makes it hard to understand. God addresses the servant directly in verse 3 by the name of Israel ('And he said to me, "You are my servant, Israel, in whom I will be glorified"'). This raises the same questions about identity that we encountered in 42:1–4. Who is the servant? Some scholars respond to the difficulty by suggesting that the word 'Israel' be removed from the text. This makes the passage much more easily read to be about an individual. The problem is that there is not a very good reason for doing this other than that it makes the text easier to read.

A more obvious solution to the problem is to say that this word is meant to be included here and, as in many other places in Isaiah, refers to God's own chosen people whom he now seeks to redeem. If this is the case, this passage is not the prophet's call narrative but the whole nation's—and also ours. This picture of being called from the mother's womb is a powerful one, speaking of how God's call is woven into the very essence of a person, not imposed on them at a later date.

God speaks here to his chosen servant(s), giving a twofold commission. The task is to restore God's chosen people and to act as a light to the nations all around so that God's salvation can reach to the ends of the earth (v. 6). Such a commission is more properly directed at the whole people of God than at a single individual. The only drawback to understanding the passage in this way is that this means that God is giving a commission to Israel to 'restore the survivors of Israel' (v. 6). Is this in fact possible? The answer to this may well be 'yes': those within a nation may be the best ones to restore their own survivors.

2 The tongue of a teacher

Isaiah 50:4–9

Isaiah 50:4–9 is regarded as the third of the four servant songs, and Isaiah continues his portrayal of the task of God's servant by introducing a new element. The servant of God will be able to teach and inspire others. Anyone who seeks to be a good teacher or who has been taught by a good teacher will recognize the description here: 'The Lord God has given me the tongue of a teacher, that I may know how to sustain the weary with a word' (v. 4). No better definition of teaching exists than to have the ability to 'sustain the weary with a word'.

The inspiration necessary for such teaching evidently comes from God as, every morning, the servant is woken 'to listen as those who are taught' (v. 4). Good teachers are in their turn taught daily by God. This is important. In a busy world it is easy to forget the importance of receiving as well as giving. The pattern of teaching that is given by this passage is that those who give must receive at least as much as they give.

The context of this verse, however, reveals how hard a task this vocation can be. The true calling of God causes the servant to suffer abuse as a part of his calling: the servant is beaten and spat at and has his beard pulled out (v. 6). Following a calling from God can often lead to suffering, as we observe most acutely at this time of year when we celebrate the fact that Jesus was prepared to die in faithful following of his calling. Servanthood here involves both good and bad, daily inspiration and physical abuse. Those who follow God's call must, like the servant here, be prepared to follow wherever the call leads.

130

Yet the promise that God gives is that God will be with those who follow in this way. This is something that the servant recognizes at the end of this passage: 'The Lord helps me; therefore I have not been disgraced' (v. 7), or, as Paul the apostle would put it, 'If God is for us, who is against us?' (Romans 8:31). Those who follow as God calls them to do have the knowledge that, whatever happens, they have a very powerful ally who will outlast anyone who opposes them (v. 9, 'It is the Lord God who helps me; who will declare me guilty? All of them will wear out like a garment; the moth will eat them up').

3 Your God reigns

Isaiah 52:7–10

The difficulty of the task of God's servant stands in contrast to the task of the messenger. The servant works patiently and gently in the world (42:1–4), restoring God's people and bringing a light to those around (49:1–6), teaching and inspiring (50:4) but also suffering abuse as a result of the task to which he is called (50:6). In contrast, even the feet of the messenger who announces peace are regarded as beautiful (v. 7). The one who brings good news is much more welcome than the one who works quietly and diligently day by day among the people.

The enthusiastic response to this messenger matches the good news that he brings. The messenger that Isaiah speaks of here announces the end of the exile. God's reign is now established and 'all the ends of the earth' see God's salvation of his people (v. 10). No wonder the messenger is greeted so well—this is good news indeed. When the exile occurred, real doubt was cast on God's reign over his people. In the ancient world, the gods were regarded as fighting on behalf of their people, so if the people were defeated, this was a symbol that their god had also been defeated by the gods of the victorious nation. This doubt was exacerbated at the exile by the destruction of the temple, God's dwelling-place on earth. If the place where God dwelt among the people was no more, surely this marked the end of God's reign?

The prophet Ezekiel answered this fear profoundly with his vision of God leaving the temple and Jerusalem on his divine chariot (Ezekiel 11:22–23). God had not been defeated: he had abandoned his people.

The message of gloom was, in a strange way, a message of hope. The destruction of the temple indicated God's abandonment of the people, not God's destruction.

No wonder, then, that the messenger who announces peace, salvation and the reign of God is greeted so enthusiastically. Messengers were generally sent ahead of a battle to announce the outcome of the battle for good or ill. This messenger is sent ahead of God to announce his victory on behalf of the people and his return. The truth of the message is borne out by the sentinels or watchmen on the city walls who 'in plain sight' see 'the return of the Lord to Zion' (v. 8).

4 Out of his anguish he shall see light

Isaiah 53:4–12

We have explored so far three out of the four passages in Isaiah which are commonly called 'the servant songs'. This passage is part of the fourth one. This 'song' is much longer than the others, encompassing a total of fifteen verses (52:13—53:12). It is also much better known. This passage is used regularly to refer to Jesus' death and possibly also to his resurrection. The use of the passage to understand Jesus has roots far back in the early Church, as it is the passage that the Ethiopian eunuch is reading in Acts 8:32–33, which Philip explains to be a reference to Jesus Christ.

This song, like the other three that we have looked at so far, is a perfect description of Jesus. Like the other three, it can also be seen to refer to the nation of Israel—or at least part of it. If the servant in this passage is understood to be the people who went into exile in Babylon, then this passage begins to make sense for Isaiah's time as much as for Jesus' time. The suffering of the servant (vv. 4–5, 7) becomes the experience of exile; being cut off from the land of the living (vv. 8–9) is like being cut off from the promised land; and seeing light out of anguish (v. 11) is the return from exile.

The question that remains, however, is how the exiles could be 'wounded for our transgressions' or how the punishment upon them 'made us whole' (v. 5). In order for this to make sense, we need to turn back to what the text actually says, rather than what centuries of

Christian interpretation have understood it to mean. The text says nothing of vicarious suffering here. The servant does not suffer instead of the people who have sinned, but as well as them. He, like they, suffered in the exile, bearing the nation's infirmities (v. 4) and suffering for their transgressions. Those in exile bore the brunt of the punishment that made the nation whole, as Isaiah tells us elsewhere (40:2). The message of hope that Isaiah offers them is that, having suffered this punishment, they can now be confident that 'they will see light' (v. 11).

God's servants are called to be alongside those who suffer, to experience with them their pain and anguish and to point beyond all of this to the light that will dawn upon them. No wonder this passage fits Jesus so well—never before had anyone fulfilled this calling as he did.

5 Come to the waters

Isaiah 55:1–5

Isaiah calls people to recognize what God has on offer for them. This passage makes clear that God will not force them to join in with the glorious new age that is now breaking forth. God issues the invitation and all must decide whether or not to accept it.

The problem seems to be that the people do not perceive the true worth of what is on offer. They prefer to spend money on that which is not bread and to work for that which does not satisfy (v. 2), instead of accepting the free gift of water, wine and milk. The image that Isaiah paints here is a vivid one. The people of God prefer to toil for an everyday phenomenon like bread—which then turns out not even to be bread—than to accept the luxury gift of wine that God offers them for free. Part of the task for those who would be true servants of God is that of discernment, of recognizing the true worth of the things around us. How often we decline God's generosity to us, preferring to concentrate on those things that we believe will sustain us but which instead turn out to have no value at all.

Isaiah goes on in verse 3 to declare what this generous, luxurious gift of God is. It is an everlasting covenant, a relationship that will go on for ever. The effect of this is that the soul, or life force, of the people will live. The NRSV does not quite do justice to what Isaiah meant here, for it translates the phrase as '*you* will live'. Isaiah means much more than this, because he uses the word *nephesh*, which is the word used in Genesis 2:7 to refer to the breath that God breathed into the nostrils of Adam. The *nephesh*, therefore, is the life force of a person, the thing that makes them who they are. It is this that will live if a person chooses to accept God's generous offer, for then they will discover life in all its fullness.

6 Seek the Lord

Isaiah 55:6–13

Isaiah 40:1–8 acts as a prologue to Isaiah 40—55. In the same way, 55:6–13 acts as an epilogue to it, since it summarizes the major theme of this part of the book to ensure that the message is hammered home.

Isaiah makes three major points. The first is an invitation to seek the Lord. During the exile, the people believed that God had abandoned them to their fate, but Isaiah now informs them that this time has passed. Now is the time to seek for God, because now he can be found. He is near to the people and if they call he will answer. This will come as something of a surprise to the exiles who believed that the temple was the place to worship God. They were unable to 'sing the Lord's song in a foreign land' (Psalm 137:4). Here Isaiah informs them that not only can they sing the Lord's song but that God will hear them and have mercy upon them (v. 7).

His second point is to remind the people of God's nature. God is not a human being; nor are his thoughts like ours. It is very easy to judge God by human standards and to assume that we can understand God's behaviour from our own behaviour. Isaiah points out how wrong this is (vv. 8–9). God can be judged only by his own standards and, as we cannot hope to understand what these are, we must accept his word which is steadfast and sure (vv. 10–11).

The result of all of this is Isaiah's third and final point: the whole earth will celebrate with the people of God as they are led out of captivity in joy and in peace. The event of the return from exile will be so momentous that even the mountains, hills and trees will celebrate its occurrence (vv. 12–13). If the people have faith in who God really is and do not judge him by human standards, and if they seek him now, then no one will be able to limit the celebration of the whole planet as God's plans for his people come to fruition.

Guidelines

People often struggle to understand the Old Testament, as it feels very alien to our Christian mindset. Isaiah 40—55, however, is much easier to read, for a very important reason. This part of Isaiah looks forward to the glorious intervention of God in the world, to a time when God would no longer be wrathful and angry but would yearn to comfort his people. Isaiah's hope is eschatological insomuch as it looks forward to a climactic moment in the future when God's presence on the earth would be felt not just in Israel but across the whole world.

One of the problems for the post-exilic community was that it did not feel as though this promise had been fulfilled. God's people remained a small, beleaguered minority on the world's stage, suffering at the hands of bigger, more powerful empires. Isaiah's glorious vision of the future did not seem to happen. Christians believe that the fulfilment of Isaiah's prophecy took place in the person of Jesus Christ, particularly in his death and resurrection. The New Testament points to the belief that Jesus' resurrection from the dead ushered in the new era that Isaiah promised so long before.

It is not surprising that Christians today find Isaiah 40—55 so valuable, for, with the resurrection of Jesus, Isaiah's promises have begun to come true. Of course, Jesus' resurrection signalled only the start of the end times—the rest is still to come. In the same way, Isaiah's promises have only started to be fulfilled—there is much more still to come. But the message of comfort, hope and joy that Isaiah proclaims is one which is planted in the hearts of all those who are 'in Christ'. God's yearning to comfort his people has at last begun to be fulfilled. God's call to us, as to the exiles, is to accept it—a simple yet extremely difficult call to answer.

Summary.

FURTHER READING

Joseph Blenkinsopp, *Isaiah 40—55* (Anchor Bible Commentary, 2002)—a well written, thoughtful commentary

Walter Brueggemann, *Isaiah 40—66* (Westminster Bible Companion, Westminster John Knox Press, 1998)—a profound and insightful commentary on the theology of Isaiah

John F.A. Sawyer, *The Fifth Gospel: Isaiah in the History of Christianity* (CUP, 1996)—expensive but worth it! A fascinating book looking at how and why Isaiah has been so important for Christianity

Guidelines

Magazine

Keeping going

Geoff Holmes

'I usually tell people that I am enjoying it, and I guess I am in some ways. At times, however, life seems intolerably painful. For instance, having to prepare a sermon brings out all my worst feelings. Have I got anything of value to say? What can I say with real integrity? Why do I have to go through this on my own? I don't think I have ever felt so lonely. Trying to give of myself just winds me up more and more. I could have hit Mrs X this morning. And yet it's not her fault really. She's just a lonely person too. I don't think I've got any answers.'

Nearly ten years on, as I browse through the ad hoc journal from which these thoughts are taken, it's hard even for me to grasp how low I felt at that time, a few months after being ordained. It's equally hard to believe that I kept going through what was probably the worst nine months of my life without giving in to the wish 'just to pack my rucksack and walk away from it all', which I also recorded a number of times.

In June 1998 I did pack my rucksack and get away from it all, but only for ten days. I wasn't giving in, I was taking on a different challenge—to walk the Pembrokeshire Coast Path from Poppit Sands to Amroth, 186 miles of official route and an overall ascent the equivalent of Everest, carrying a tent, cooking equipment and as little clothing and food as possible.

The highlights were spectacular—the dramatic cliffs with their folds and fissures of rock, the desolate headlands and intimate village ports; the richness of the wild flowers that grow in such profusion, the flight and call of the sea birds; the feelings of simplicity and well-being and the constant presence of the great interface between sky, land and sea where an ever-changing drama is enacted day and night. The low points were agonizing—blisters, blisters and more blisters; and with them the threat of giving up,

…the constant presence of the great interface between sky, land and sea…

which would mean disappointment and failure.

It wasn't that I was unprepared. I had trained well in the previous weeks, doing progressively longer distances with a heavier pack, but my favourite boots had more or less collapsed on me the previous Monday and I was wearing a rather heavy and inflexible pair that I hadn't put on for two years. It was only after I jettisoned them for a pair of high-performance sandals halfway through the walk that things began to look up on that front.

As an Anglican priest, the system I work within doesn't always feel very flexible. The baggage of centuries—buildings, liturgy, outdated expectations—can wear you down and sap your strength. Much of this heritage is good in its own way and that just makes the equation harder to solve. Within all this, you have to try to find your own flexible and creative ways of working, ways that are lightweight and responsive. Above all, you have to find your 'heart' and go with it; otherwise you will be flogging a dead animal, only to discover that animal is you!

I tried to make my Pembrokeshire walk a pilgrimage for renewing my heart—finding the 'treasure in jars of clay'. My morning prayer was from the hymn of St Patrick:

I arise today through a mighty strength
the strong name of the Trinity
through belief in the threeness
through the confession of the oneness
of the creator of creation.

I first started using this morning prayer in those lonely days as a curate. I still associate it strongly with the shower in the house where I lived then. The words couldn't have been more at odds with the feelings inside and yet, in the awareness and acceptance of that fissure in myself, I began to find a new strength of spirituality.

Mornings on the coast path saw me make my tea and cook my porridge, strike camp and put everything I needed on my back, say goodbye to another resting place and set out to conquer the miles ahead, not certain that I would, but finding strength in the beauty of all that was around me. Religious practice can easily settle around ideas and experiences that have actually lost their evocative power. True faith is a process of risk, and only through risk can we discover anew the real strength that comes from God.

> *Only through risk can we discover anew the real strength that comes from God*

One of the roughest and most desolate parts of the walk was across Strumble Head. I had camped at the tiny bay of Porthsych, stamping a pitch for my tent out of the undergrowth before making a bonfire and singing to the seals that had come in to watch. Having set off early the next morning, I looked forward to a second breakfast at the Pwllderi Youth Hostel. Unfortunately it was shut, so no bacon, eggs, sausage, beans and no chance to stock up on provisions. Feeling disheartened and rapidly running out of energy, I managed to make it, emptily and painfully, to Trefin where I ordered soup and a roll, and a whole dressed crab salad with chips. I ate every scrap, and then all the butter and sauces, before stocking up at the shop and eating further a packet of yoghurt-coated nuts and raisins and a third of a packet of chocolate Hobnobs.

If walking blows out the cobwebs and gives a sense of achievement, it also begins to reveal our humanity. We are so used to being well fed that it's a strange experience to literally run out of energy and then feel revived by a chocolate bar or banana. In a similar way, during my early days in ministry— when I was near enough parachuted into a parish where my life effectively began again from scratch—I discovered what it was like to have no emotional resource or support. I also discovered the impossibility of existing, let alone ministering, on such a basis. We need friendship; we need familiar places and habits that give our lives structure and a sense of meaning and belonging. Perhaps 90 per cent of unacknowledged spirituality actually lies in these everyday things.

My afternoon prayer was from a favourite hymn:

Be thou my vision,
O Lord of my heart
Naught be all else to me
save that thou art
Thou my best thought
in the day and the night
Both waking and sleeping,
Thy presence my light.

It was early afternoon when I arrived at the little chapel of St Non (St Non was the mother of St David and he was born nearby during a great storm in AD462). The little chapel, built in the Celtic style, was peaceful and cool in contrast to the burning sun outside. I lit a candle and mused on the fact that the God present to me there was the same God of the cliffs, the winds and the sea. Later, I decided

> *We need familiar places and habits that give our lives structure*

that I preferred that little building to St David's Cathedral, which was impressive but full of tourists and tour parties. In the cathedral, for all its grandeur, I didn't seem to find the 'heart' that I did with my little candle in St Non's.

One of the main problems of my early days as a curate was that I hadn't found my 'heart', or at least I didn't really trust it as the place where God could meet me. Each week I searched for the perfect sermon, which was, of course, miles beyond me. I tried to give because I felt it was expected, when actually I had 'nothing in the tank'. It wasn't until I gave myself a break and started to be kind to myself, to trust myself and build on my own sense of integrity that I began to feel free to speak and give and feel that it was all worthwhile.

I did manage to keep going and complete the walk, and I count it in various ways as one of my greatest achievements. Something I ought to go on thinking about is whether I would have been a failure if I hadn't completed it. Being driven gets things done, but perhaps it needs to be balanced by good sense! In any case, we can't escape the wider perspective, which keeps us humble. I remember the lump in my throat when

> *I began to feel free to speak and give and feel that it was all worthwhile*

for the first time I rounded a headland and saw the coast beyond Amroth where my walk would finish. For the first time I couldn't say to myself, 'That's where I'll be tomorrow.' The coast would go on but my involvement with it would be over.

Life and ministry belong to God. We play a part in it, but only a part. The knowledge that it is bigger than us can set us free to live to the full and make the most of what we have been given.

Geoff Holmes is Vicar of Worsbrough St Thomas & St James in South Yorkshire and is married to Rebecca with two daughters, Imogen and Jemima. A full diary of his coast path walk is available from geoffrey.r.holmes@tesco.net

An extract from
Jacob and the Prodigal

Israel, the community to which Jesus belonged, took its name from the patriarch Jacob. His story of exile and return was their story as well. *Jacob and the Prodigal* examines the well-known parable of the prodigal son, and shows how, in telling it, Jesus took the story of Jacob and reshaped it in his own way and for his own purposes. In writing this comparative study of the Old Testament family saga and the New Testament parable, Kenneth Bailey draws on a lifetime of study in Middle Eastern culture, the Gospels and, in particular, the parable of the prodigal son. The following extract is from Chapter 15 (abridged).

Two Dancers in a Single Dance

Reflections on N.T. Wright's Interpretation of the Parable of the Prodigal Son

In his monumental work *Jesus and the Victory of God*, N.T. Wright discusses the parable of the prodigal son in a thought-provoking and stimulating manner. Because of the broad scope of what he has written, it is difficult, if not impossible, to interact adequately with the many theological echoes that reverberate on numerous levels from his reflections. However, a few brief remarks may be useful to the continuing wider discussion.

Wright's main thesis, regarding the parable of the prodigal son, is that it is a story of 'exile and return' that is 'designed to blow apart the normal first-century reading of Jewish history and to replace it with a different one'. Israel's history in both the exodus and the exile was a story of 'exile and return', and the prodigal is a symbol of that same classical movement. In the parable, Wright argues, the real exile and return occurs in Jesus' own ministry…

Wright's call for a 'criterion of double similarity' needs to be taken with utmost seriousness. He argues that when an understanding of Gospel texts fits into the world of first-century Judaism and at the same time functions 'credibly as the implied starting point (though not the exact replica) of something in later Christianity, [there] is a strong possibility of our being in touch with the genuine history of Jesus'.

…The concern of this work is the theology of Jesus in his first-century Jewish setting. This Jesuic starting point is demonstrably the foundation of early Christianity. No one is more completely saved by grace (the message of the Epistle to the Romans) than the prodigal son. But the developing Christian theology of the Epistles and of the Gospel historians and theologians is beyond the focus of this inquiry. Yet, within the limits of this quest, it is appropriate to ask two related questions:

(a) What does Jesus say in this parable to individuals and groups of listeners as he answers the Pharisees' complaint, 'This man receives sinners and eats with them'?

(b) Is Jesus also talking to Israel as a whole as he creates this parable, and, if so, what is he saying to the nation?

…On the level of lawkeeping and lawbreaking sinners, Jesus presents two points of view:

- The prodigal (in the far country) says, 'I will work and pay—and everything can thereby be made right.'
- The older son says, 'I have worked and I have obeyed, and everything is fine as long as my standards are maintained.'

Both are wrong, and both are lost and in 'exile'. The father must pay a high price to restore each of his sons. This applies on the personal level and at the level of the various parties around Jesus, such as the scribes, the Pharisees and the 'people of the land'. Yet the parable also has a wider application as it depicts the crisis of the nation, as Wright has so ably argued.

But Israel is not merely *the prodigal* returning home from exile. Israel includes two sons, both of whom start 'in the field'. Each moves toward the house. Each, at some point, defines his relationship to the father as that of a servant. Each breaks his relationship with the father on a very deep level. The father suffers to reconcile each. Both must accept being found, for only then can the real return from exile be accomplished. Their exile is not from the land but from their father's heart. The prodigal is still in exile at the edge of the village while the older son is in exile in the courtyard of the house. The prodigal's return 'from the field' with the

> *The father must pay a high price to restore each of his sons*

pigs means nothing if, at the edge of the village, he insists on becoming a paid craftsman and thereby refuses to be found and brought from death to life. Likewise, the return of the older son 'from the field' signifies nothing if he refuses to accept his father's love and continues his 'exile' in the courtyard of the family home.

As noted, Jesus is addressing not only individuals and groups within the community, like the Pharisees, but the nation as well. Both the saga of Jacob and the parable of the compassionate father deal with a family. Genesis 27:1—36:8 focuses on a father and two sons, as does the parable. Each text is deeply concerned for the entire family. Thus the topic of the significance of Jesus' parable for the nation requires investigation.

Wright investigates the importance of the parable for the nation. He sees this story as applying both to the exodus (the sojourn in Egypt and the return from Egypt) and to the exile (the captivity in Babylon and the return from that captivity). He writes:

The exodus itself is the ultimate backdrop; Israel goes off into a pagan country, becomes a slave, then is brought back to her own land. But exile and restoration is the main theme. This is what the parable is about.

I readily grant that exile and return is the main theme of the parable of the two lost sons. But any attempt at finding too close a parallel (or a set of parallels) between the exodus, the exile and the parable creates problems for interpretation. Jacob and his family migrated to Egypt because of a famine. They did not leave their homeland under a cloud of sin related to tensions and ambitions within the family, as did the prodigal and Jacob. They were not driven into exile by God because of their worship of idols.

Too close a tie between the parable and the details of the exodus further complicates the overall interpretation of the parable. Wright suggests that the older son (who opposes the prodigal's acceptance at home) can be identified with Pharaoh (who tries to stop Israel from returning home). But the older son did not try to stop the prodigal from leaving the far country as Pharaoh attempted to do with Israel. Such a part could easily have been played by the citizen in the far country who hired the prodigal to feed his pigs. That citizen could have come on stage and done his best to prevent the prodigal from starting home. Said citizen would understandably not want to lose a pig herder whom he does not have to pay, but unlike Pharaoh the citizen does not oppose the prodigal's return. In fact no one attempts to stop him…

The authenticity of the prodigal's repentance in the far country is a further difficulty. Wright observes, 'When, therefore, Israel comes to her senses, and returns with all her heart, there is an astonishing, prodigal, lavish welcome waiting for her.' This assumes that the phrase 'he came to himself' (Lk. 15:17), used to describe the prodigal in the far country, is authentic repentance as taught by Jesus. As I have argued at length in this study, if this be the case, then the parables of the lost sheep and the lost coin are false presentations of Jesus' views. In both of those stories the key figure must work hard to find the lost. The lost do not come home of their own accord.

Does the third story (the parable of the prodigal son) contradict the two parables that immediately precede it? Surely not. Rather, the parable of the prodigal son presents two views of repentance. The first is the audience's view of repentance, which Jesus shows to be inauthentic. The second is the new, authentic view he presents. The audience's perception is demonstrated by the prodigal in the far country, who in effect says:

I will solve my own problem. I will apologize, get job training, become a skilled craftsman, earn money and pay back what I have lost. My only problem is a cashflow shortage and the resulting fact that I am starving.

The parable of the prodigal son presents two views of repentance

The second view of repentance is presented at the edge of the village, where a costly demonstration of unexpected love breaks through to the prodigal, who at long last realizes that money is not the issue. When he sees his father getting hurt for him, he suddenly discovers that he has a broken relationship that needs restoration. He 'accepts being found' by costly love, and a new world opens that can only be adequately described with the language of resurrection. This resurrection does not take place in the far country. It happens at the edge of the village when he accepts the unqualified grace offered to him by his father. As he arrives at the edge of the village, the prodigal is still in exile!

Jubilees rewrote the saga of Jacob, as did Josephus. The rabbis commented on the fixed text. Philo chose to philosophize on it. Jesus writes a new story, but that new tale reuses, revises and reverses primary elements from the old. As regards 'exile and return', I would suggest that Wright is correct in observing that Jesus' parable relates to that classical movement. Perhaps it is helpful to see four distinct journeys of exile and return, each with its own unique elements. These are:

- Out of fear Jacob goes into *exile to Haran* and *returns to Succoth*.
- Jacob's family *migrates to Egypt* because of famine, and centuries later, with God's help, *returns* at the time of *the exodus*.
- Israel is driven by God into *exile in Babylon*, and a part of the community *returns under Cyrus*.
- Jesus tells a new story about exile and return, and those around him hear this story as a *unique addition* to this series, an addition that is fashioned out of the saga of Jacob. They also understand this new story as containing a description of his own person and mission.

Naturally, the 'unique addition' has a new twist. Wright correctly affirms, 'The real return from exile... is taking place, in an extremely paradoxical fashion, in Jesus' own ministry'.

It is clear that for Jesus the problem for the nation is not simply a matter of unfulfilled 'perks' of restoration promised by the prophets to the people on their return from exile. Rather Jesus sees the Essenes, Pharisees, scribes and indeed Zealots on one side taking the law very, very seriously. He also sees the 'people of the land', who were slack about the law and thus despised, on the other side. Both groups assumed that their physical presence in the land demonstrated that they had already returned from exile. Jesus' new 'exile and return' vision thunders at them:

Both of you are still in exile! Both of you are sinners! Both of you live unreconciled to God! The divine presence of God is with you in me, and I am among you calling on you to be reconciled to him. I am eager to welcome and eat with both kinds of sinners. I will eat with Simon the Pharisee and in his presence defend a sinful woman who makes up for his mistakes. I will also eat with Matthew the tax collector and his friends. I am among you in the landowner who pays all workers a living wage irrespective of how long they have worked. When you accept being found by my costly love, you are authentically brought back from your real exile, and the lost are found and the dead brought to life as you are reconciled to God.

As Wright eloquently says:

In telling this story, he [Jesus] is explaining and vindicating his own practice of eating with sinners; his celebratory meals are the equivalent, in real life, of the homecoming party in the story. They are the celebration of the return from exile. What is more, Jesus is claiming that, when he does all this, Israel's god is doing it, welcoming sinners no matter whether they have passed all the normal tests for membership, as long as they will accept the welcome of Jesus.

To this statement I would only suggest one emendation. The banquet in the parable is perhaps better described as a celebration of 'restoration from exile'. This 'restoration from exile' occurs at the edge of the village and is accomplished by the father (as the father and the young boy in the parable make clear). Also, the parable affirms that the state of exile applies to the older son as much as it does to the younger. The extraordinary efforts of the father before and during the celebration are directed first to one son and then to the other in heroic attempts at bringing both sons back from exile, and at restoring each from death to life.

Jesus is indeed addressing the entire nation. As noted, both lawkeepers and lawbreakers are in exile. He goes to them in their exile and is willing finally to pay the ultimate price of his own life to bring them back from exile.

The parable of the lost sheep has the same basic dynamics. There are three elements in the story: a flock, a shepherd and a lost sheep. It is impossible to imagine that the shepherd is indifferent to the fate of the entire flock. In the parable he carries the lost sheep back to the village. The story stops with the ninety-nine still 'in the wilderness'. The listener instinctively asks, 'Isn't the shepherd going to go after them as well?' The answer to this question appears in the third story when the father first 'brings back' the lost younger son and then does his best to rescue the older son. Together they are the flock/Israel/ the family. Getting the family together/at home/at the banquet table with him is his goal. This is the authentic return from exile.

The looming battle with Rome is misguided. Among the twelve apostles Jesus includes a tax collector (the worst of sinners) and a Zealot (the most aggressive of the lawkeepers). This is by choice! There is no hint anywhere in the Gospel tradition that these two were not reconciled. Jesus' new vision of exile and return can save the nation by redirecting its energies to its real problem, which is its exile from God. When his solution is not accepted by the majority, he knows the result will be tragic for the nation. He is fully able to 'interpret the present time' (Lk. 12:56). This awareness leads him to weep over Jerusalem, to prophesy against her and, on the way to his cross, to warn the women of the terrible inevitable consequences of the nation's rejection of his solution to its continued exile from God.

'Exile and return' is indeed a paradigm at the heart of Jesus' message—for the individual, for groups within the nation and for the nation itself. Jesus speaks to all three in this parable, which is newly created on the foundation of the saga of Jacob and is, at the same time, a new addition to the classical historical episodes of exile and return experienced in the exodus and in the exile…

To order a copy of this book, please turn to page 159.

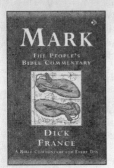

MARK

THE PEOPLE'S
BIBLE COMMENTARY

DICK
FRANCE

A BIBLE COMMENTARY FOR EVERY DAY

The People's Bible Commentary

Mark's Gospel is the shortest of the four books telling the story of Jesus of Nazareth, yet it is the most vividly told. The writer shows the disconcerting influence of Jesus on his often bewildered disciples, and how their world was turned upside down by the values of the kingdom of God, amidst scenes of eager crowds, dramatic confrontations and impressive miracles. The commentary is written by the Revd Dr Dick France, who has also written PBC Timothy, Titus and Hebrews.

MARK 14:1–2, 10–11

THE PRIESTS & JUDAS ISCARIOT

The plot against Jesus

We have had plenty of indications of how the religious authorities are reacting to Jesus. Even as far back as Mark 3:6 they were plotting his death. Now he is in Jerusalem, within their grasp, and the time has come. But the same Passover festival which has brought Jesus to Jerusalem has also brought thousands of other pilgrims to the temple, and many of them already know Jesus, and are his enthusiastic supporters—as the pilgrim crowds have demonstrated when they escorted him into the city with shouts of 'Hosanna'. To make an open move against Jesus would be likely to provoke a riot.

During the day, Jesus spent his time in the temple, very publicly. The only answer, then, is to try to arrest him at night, when there are no crowds of supporters around. But how do you find one among 100,000 Passover visitors? The city was far too small for the crowds who came at festival time, and the visitors spread out to the surrounding villages or camped on the hillsides around the city. They must find inside information of where Jesus and his disciples are staying.

The informer

And that is where Judas comes in. His betrayal of Jesus consists firstly in his willingness to tell the authorities where the disciple group may be found at night, and indeed, as we shall see, to lead them there in person and identify Jesus so that they can arrest him. This is the service they most need from him, and it is for this that he is to be well paid. We shall see also, however, that when Jesus is brought to trial, the high priest will be well informed about the sort of things Jesus has been saying about himself and his mission. Since most of the relevant sayings have been uttered in private to the disciples, it seems likely that it is Judas who has fed the authorities with appropriate evidence which they can use against Jesus when the time comes.

Why did he do it?

It has always seemed incredible that a man who has devoted a year or more of his life to following Jesus could suddenly turn against him in this way. Few have been able to believe that a cash payment would alone be enough to motivate such a radical decision. Beyond that, we are in the area of conjecture.

One interesting fact is that Judas' name, Iscariot, may indicate that he came from a town, Keriot, in southern Judea. If so, that would probably mean that he was the only non-Galilean among the Twelve. So he may have come to feel out of place in this Galilean movement, and the more so when the group has come down to Judea, and the Galilean crowds have welcomed 'their' prophet into the capital. So perhaps there is an element of racial prejudice in Judas' decision.

But it is likely that there is a more fundamental reason than that. As they have journeyed towards Jerusalem, Jesus has again and again made it quite plain to his disciples that he has no intention, as many had hoped, of leading a movement to restore Israel's national independence; his mission is not to lead his people to victory but to be rejected and die. Peter's remonstrance against such an idea (8:32) would have been echoed by the other disciples, and they have followed him reluctantly and with bewilderment.

If Judas originally joined the movement for motives of high-minded patriotism, he will have watched with dismay as Jesus has stubbornly rejected any such mission. And now in Jerusalem Jesus has made matters worse by actually attacking the temple itself, the very symbol of national pride, and daring to predict its destruction. Judas' desertion would then have been the result of disillusionment: this is not the sort of movement he had thought he was joining. His approach to the priests would then be partly an attempt to save his own skin while there is still time; but it might also arise from a genuine conviction that Jesus has embarked on a dangerous and unpatriotic course, and must be stopped before he does any more harm.

For meditation

If you think you are standing, watch out that you do not fall.

Recommended reading

God of the Valley
by Steve Griffiths

This book deals with the painful subjects of grief and suffering, but it is neither a simple personal testimony nor a volume of theological theory. *God of the Valley* combines a deeply personal story with searching—ransacking, even—Scripture to find answers to the hardest of questions, to find consolation in the darkest of times and, ultimately, to find hope.

The introduction sets the scene in dramatic fashion. Steve, a newly ordained church minister recently settled with his family in a new parish, comes home to find his wife, Clare, suffering an agonizing migraine. In a matter of weeks she is diagnosed with a massive brain tumour. Radical treatment means that she eventually survives another eight years, dying at the age of 36. During the same period, Steve also loses his sister, his best friend, his grandfather and Clare's grandmother in a relatively short space of time.

He begins the book with what he acknowledges as the toughest question of all—'why?'—and shows how the Wisdom literature in the Bible (particularly Job and Ecclesiastes) do not provide comfortable answers that may deny the reality of pain, but reveal to us the sovereignty of God and how we need to learn to rest in a 'cloud of unknowing'.

With searing honesty he describes the range of emotions that characterized those eight years for him, including the mixture of feelings he went through while caring for Clare, from anguish at her suffering to frustration with her limitations, which in turn led to guilt.

Recalling a pilgrimage they were able to make to the Holy Land, he tells of their visit to Bethany, the scene of the raising of Lazarus. At the time, he imagined the crowd waiting to see whether anything would happen after Jesus called his dead friend to 'come out'. Later, he reflected on how he had spent eight years waiting for Jesus to heal Clare miraculously. After trying every conceivable form of prayer, he eventually realized that he had to learn to trust in the grace and love of God.

He shares in vivid detail the morning when he said his final goodbyes to Clare in hospital, the shocking pain he felt immediately after she died, and the complete exhaustion and emptiness that characterized the ensuing weeks and months. He speaks of the silence of grief—and coping with the assumptions of others that he must be 'getting over it' because he was not grieving in a visible way.

He describes the challenge of shaping a new identity after years of being 'SteveandClare'; of caring for his young daughter in the midst of it all; of how he had to acknowledge his deep anger at what had happened, before God could deal with it. And he movingly describes the sense that his ministry was over, that he had nothing worthwhile left to say to anybody, but how God could still 'restore his soul'.

This book provides invaluable insights for those who want to understand more of the experiences of suffering and bereavement, and shows those in the middle of such experiences—or facing the prospect of them—that while each situation is as unique as the individuals concerned, they are not alone. God brings healing, although not necessarily in the way they may have originally hoped or expected.

As well as being a Church of England minister, now based in Essex, Dr Steve Griffiths is a tutor at the Centre for Youth Ministry at Ridley Hall in Cambridge, and Chief Editor of *The Journal of Youth and Theology*. His teaching ministry has taken him to South Africa, the USA and India and he has written books and articles on theology, youth ministry and church history.

In *God of the Valley*, however, he writes not as a lecturer, a counsellor or even an experienced church minister, but as somebody who has found himself strengthened and comforted by God. He writes how ultimately we can do nothing except cling on to God, who alone offers the hope of restoration.

The subtitle of the book, 'A journey through grief', summarizes its concluding message. Yes, suffering and bereavement are devastating, leaving us bereft of spiritual and emotional reserves, but they are nevertheless part of a journey. Grief may seem like a bottomless pit, but in the love of God we can discover a way through, back to the light. The introduction to the ten chapters of *God of the Valley* is entitled 'A story of pain' but the conclusion is headed 'Two stories of redemption'.

The foreword, by Canon David Winter, sums it up well: 'This is truth through story, through poetry, through the experience of God's people down the ages. It shows us how the Bible can speak with peculiar power and relevance to our own experience of personal loss. And it is full of Christian hope.'

To order a copy of this book, turn to page 159.

For reflection

The dark night of the soul

During the time... of the aridities of this night of sense, spiritual persons suffer great trials, by reason not so much of the aridities which they suffer, as of the fear which they have of being lost on the road, thinking that all spiritual blessing is over for them and that God has abandoned them since they find no help or pleasure in good things. Then they grow weary, and endeavour (as they have been accustomed to do) to concentrate their faculties with some degree of pleasure upon some object of meditation... This effort they make not without great inward repugnance and unwillingness on the part of their soul, which was taking pleasure in being in that quietness and ease, instead of working with its faculties...

These souls turn back at such a time if there is none who understands them; they abandon the road or lose courage; or, at the least, they are hindered from going farther by the great trouble which they take in advancing along the road of meditation and reasoning. Thus they fatigue and overwork their nature, imagining that they are failing through negligence or sin. But this trouble that they are taking is quite useless, for God is now leading them by another road, which is that of contemplation, and is very different from the first; for the one is of meditation and reasoning, and the other belongs neither to imagination nor yet to reasoning.

It is well for those who find themselves in this condition to take comfort, to persevere in patience and to be in no wise afflicted. Let them trust in God, Who abandons not those that seek Him with a simple and right heart, and will not fail to give them what is needful for the road, until He bring them into the clear and pure light of love...

The way in which they are to conduct themselves in this night of sense is to devote themselves not at all to reasoning and meditation, since this is not the time for it, but to allow the soul to remain in peace and quietness, although it may seem clear to them that they are doing nothing and are wasting their time, and although it may appear to them that it is because of their weakness that they have no desire in that state to think of anything. The truth is that they will be doing quite sufficient if they have patience and persevere in prayer without making any effort. What they must do is merely to leave the soul free and disencumbered and at rest from all knowledge and thought, troubling not themselves, in that state, about what they shall think or meditate upon, but contenting themselves with merely a peaceful and loving attentiveness toward God, and in being without anxiety, without the ability and without desire to have experience of Him or to perceive Him. For all these yearnings disquiet and distract the soul from the peaceful quiet and sweet ease of contemplation which is here granted to it.

And although further scruples may come to them—that they are wasting their time, and that it would be well for them to do something else, because they can neither do nor think anything in prayer—let them suffer these scruples and remain in peace, as there is no question save of their being at ease and having freedom of spirit. For if such a soul should desire to make any effort of its own with its interior faculties, this means that it will hinder and lose the blessings which, by means of that peace and ease of the soul, God is instilling into it and impressing upon it. It is just as if some painter were painting or dyeing a face; if the sitter were to move because he desired to do something, he would prevent the painter from accomplishing anything and would disturb him in what he was doing... For the more a soul endeavours to find support in affection and knowledge, the more will it feel the lack of these, which cannot now be supplied to it upon that road.

Wherefore it behoves such a soul to pay no heed if the operations of its faculties become lost to it; it is rather to desire that this should happen quickly. For, by not hindering the operation of infused contemplation that God is bestowing upon it, it can receive this with more peaceful abundance, and cause its spirit to be enkindled and to burn with the love which this dark and secret contemplation brings with it and sets firmly in the soul. For contemplation is naught else than a secret, peaceful and loving infusion from God, which, if it be permitted, enkindles the soul with the spirit of love...

Contemplation is naught else than a secret, peaceful and loving infusion from God

John of the Cross (1542–91), *Dark Night of the Soul*, Book I chapter 10 (abridged)

Guidelines © BRF 2004

The Bible Reading Fellowship
First Floor, Elsfield Hall, 15–17 Elsfield Way, Oxford OX2 8FG
ISBN 1 84101 232 7

Distributed in Australia by:
Willow Connection, PO Box 288, Brookvale, NSW 2100.
Tel: 02 9948 3957; Fax: 02 9948 8153;
E-mail: info@willowconnection.com.au
Available also from all good Christian bookshops in Australia.
For individual and group subscriptions in Australia:
Mrs Rosemary Morrall, PO Box W35, Wanniassa, ACT 2903.

Distributed in New Zealand by:
Scripture Union Wholesale, PO Box 760, Wellington
Tel: 04 385 0421; Fax: 04 384 3990; E-mail: suwholesale@clear.net.nz

Distributed in South Africa by:
Struik Book Distributors, PO Box 1144, Cape Town 8000
Tel: 021 462 4630; Fax: 021 461 3612; E-mail: enquiry@struik.co.za

Publications distributed to more than 60 countries

Acknowledgments

Cover picture: Rotunda interior of Old Illinois State Capitol, Springfield, USA

Printed in Denmark

BRF seeks to help people of all ages to experience the living God—Father, Son and Holy Spirit—at a deeper level, and enable them to grow as disciples of Jesus Christ through the Bible, prayer and worship.

We need your help if we are to make a real impact on the local church and community. In an increasingly secular world people need even more help with their Bible reading, their prayer and their discipleship. We can do something about this, but our resources are limited. With your help, if we all do a little, together we can make a huge difference.

How can you help?

- You could become a *Friend of BRF* and encourage BRF's ministry within your own church and community (contact the BRF office, or visit the BRF website, www.brf.org.uk).

- You could support BRF's ministry with a donation or standing order (using the response form overleaf).

- You could consider making a bequest to BRF in your will, and so give lasting support to our work. (We have a leaflet available with more information about this, which can be requested using the form overleaf.)

- And, most important of all, you could become a BRF *Prayer Partner* and support BRF with your prayers. *Prayer Partners* receive our bi-monthly prayer letter which includes details of all that is going on within BRF and specific prayer pointers for each prayer need. (To become a *Prayer Partner* write to BRF or e-mail enquiriesr@brf.org.uk)

Whatever you can do or give, we thank you for your support.

BRF MINISTRY APPEAL RESPONSE FORM

Name _____

Address _____

_____ Postcode _____

Telephone _____ Email _____

(tick as appropriate)

Gift Aid Declaration

☐ I am a UK taxpayer. I want BRF to treat as Gift Aid Donations all donations I make from 6 April 2000 until I notify you otherwise.

Signature _____ Date _____

☐ I would like to support BRF's ministry with a regular donation by standing order (please complete the Banker's Order below).

Standing Order – Banker's Order

To the Manager, Name of Bank/Building Society _____

Address _____

_____ Postcode _____

Sort Code _____ Account Name _____

Account No _____

Please pay Royal Bank of Scotland plc, London Drummonds Branch, 49 Charing Cross, London SW1A 2DX (Sort Code 16-00-38), for the account of BRF A/C No. 00774151

The sum of _____ pounds on ___ /____ /____ (insert date your standing order starts) and thereafter the same amount on the same day of each month until further notice.

Signature _____ Date _____

Single donation

☐ I enclose my cheque/credit card/Switch card details for a donation of £5 £10 £25 £50 £100 £250 (other) £ _____ to support BRF's ministry

Credit/ Switch card no. ☐☐☐☐☐☐☐☐☐☐☐☐☐☐☐☐☐☐☐☐

Expires ☐☐ ☐☐ ☐☐   Issue no. of Switch card ☐☐☐

Signature _____ Date _____

(Where appropriate, on receipt of your donation, we will send you a Gift Aid form)

☐ Please send me information about making a bequest to BRF in my will.

Please detach and send this completed form to: Richard Fisher, BRF, First Floor, Elsfield Hall, 15–17 Elsfield Way, Oxford OX2 8FG. BRF is a Registered Charity (No.233280)

GUIDELINES SUBSCRIPTIONS

Please note our subscription rates 2004–2005. From the May 2004 issue, the new subscription rates will be:

Individual subscriptions covering 3 issues for under 5 copies, payable in advance (including postage and packing):

		UK	SURFACE	AIRMAIL
GUIDELINES each set of 3 p.a.		£11.40	£12.75	£15.00
GUIDELINES 3-year sub	i.e. 9 issues	£28.95	N/A	N/A

Group subscriptions covering 3 issues for 5 copies or more, sent to ONE address (post free):

GUIDELINES	£9.45	each set of 3 p.a.

Please note that the annual billing period for Group Subscriptions runs from 1 May to 30 April.

Copies of the notes may also be obtained from Christian bookshops:

GUIDELINES	£3.15 each copy

GUIDELINES SUBSCRIPTIONS

❏ I would like to give a gift subscription (please complete both name and address sections below)

❏ I would like to take out a subscription myself (complete name and address details only once)

This completed coupon should be sent with appropriate payment to BRF. Alternatively, please write to us quoting your name, address, the subscription you would like for either yourself or a friend (with their name and address), the start date and credit card number, expiry date and signature if paying by credit card.

Gift subscription name _____

Gift subscription address _____

_____Postcode _____

Please send beginning with the May / September 2004 / January 2005 issue: (delete as applicable)

(please tick box)	UK	SURFACE	AIR MAIL
GUIDELINES	❏ £11.40	❏ £12.75	❏ £15.00
GUIDELINES 3-year sub	❏ £28.95		

Please complete the payment details below and send your coupon, with appropriate payment to: **BRF, First Floor, Elsfield Hall, 15–17 Elsfield Way, Oxford OX2 8FG.**

Your name _____

Your address _____

_____Postcode _____

Total enclosed £ _____ (cheques should be made payable to 'BRF')

Payment by cheque ❏ postal order ❏ Visa ❏ Mastercard ❏ Switch ❏

Card number: ⬚⬚⬚⬚ ⬚⬚⬚⬚ ⬚⬚⬚⬚ ⬚⬚⬚⬚ ⬚⬚⬚⬚

Expiry date of card: ⬚⬚⬚⬚   Issue number (Switch): ⬚⬚⬚⬚

Signature (essential if paying by credit/Switch card) _____

❏ Please do not send me further information about BRF publications.

Please ensure that you complete and send off both sides of this order form.

Please send me the following book(s):

		Quantity	Price	Total
358 7	Jacob and the Prodigal (K. Bailey)	_____	£12.99	_____
338 2	God of the Valley (S. Griffiths)	_____	£6.99	_____
334 X	The Harmony of Heaven (G. Giles)	_____	£7.99	_____
325 0	Things that Go Bump in the Night (P. Privett)	_____	£7.99	_____
348 X	Easter Make and Do (G. Chapman)	_____	£5.99	_____
192 4	PBC: Leviticus and Numbers (M. Butterworth)	_____	£7.99	_____
095 2	PBC: Joshua and Judges (S. Mathewson)	_____	£7.99	_____
030 8	PBC: 1 & 2 Samuel (H. Mowvley)	_____	£7.99	_____
118 5	PBC: 1 & 2 Kings (S. Dawes)	_____	£7.99	_____
070 7	PBC: Chronicles—Nehemiah (M. Tunnicliffe)	_____	£7.99	_____
094 4	PBC: Job (K. Dell)	_____	£7.99	_____
031 6	PBC: Psalms 1—72 (D. Coggan)	_____	£7.99	_____
065 0	PBC: Psalms 73—150 (D. Coggan)	_____	£7.99	_____
071 5	PBC: Proverbs (E. Mellor)	_____	£7.99	_____
087 1	PBC: Jeremiah (R. Mason)	_____	£7.99	_____
040 5	PBC: Ezekiel (E. Lucas)	_____	£7.99	_____
028 6	PBC: Nahum—Malachi (G. Emmerson)	_____	£7.99	_____
191 6	PBC: Matthew (J. Proctor)	_____	£7.99	_____
046 4	PBC: Mark (D. France)	_____	£7.99	_____
027 8	PBC: Luke (H. Wansbrough)	_____	£7.99	_____
029 4	PBC: John (R.A. Burridge)	_____	£7.99	_____
082 0	PBC: Romans (J. Dunn)	_____	£7.99	_____
122 3	PBC: 1 Corinthians (J. Murphy-O'Connor)	_____	£7.99	_____
073 1	PBC: 2 Corinthians (A. Besançon Spencer)	_____	£7.99	_____
012 X	PBC: Galatians and 1 & 2 Thessalonians (J. Fenton)	_____	£7.99	_____
047 2	PBC: Ephesians—Colossians & Philemon (M. Maxwell)	_____	£7.99	_____
119 3	PBC: Timothy, Titus and Hebrews (D. France)	_____	£7.99	_____
092 8	PBC: James—Jude (F. Moloney)	_____	£7.99	_____

Total cost of books £ _____

Postage and packing (see over) £ _____

TOTAL £ _____

See over for payment details. All prices are correct at time of going to press, are subject to the prevailing rate of VAT and may be subject to change without prior warning.

The Bible Reading Fellowship is a Registered Charity

PAYMENT DETAILS

Please complete the payment details below and send with appropriate payment and completed order form to:

**BRF, First Floor, Elsfield Hall,
15–17 Elsfield Way, Oxford OX2 8FG**

Name _____

Address _____

_____

_____ Postcode _____

Telephone _____

Email _____

Total enclosed £ _____ (cheques should be made payable to 'BRF')

Payment by cheque ❑ postal order ❑ Visa ❑ Mastercard ❑ Switch ❑

Card number: ☐☐☐☐☐☐☐☐☐☐☐☐☐☐☐☐☐☐☐

Expiry date of card: ☐☐☐☐   Issue number (Switch): ☐☐☐☐

Signature (essential if paying by credit/Switch card) _____

ALTERNATIVE WAYS TO ORDER

Christian bookshops: All good Christian bookshops stock BRF publications. For your nearest stockist, please contact BRF.

POSTAGE AND PACKING CHARGES				
order value	UK	Europe	Surface	Air Mail
£7.00 & under	£1.25	£3.00	£3.50	£5.50
£7.01–£30.00	£2.25	£5.50	£6.50	£10.00
Over £30.00	free	prices on request		

Telephone: The BRF office is open between 09.15 and 17.00.
To place your order, phone 01865 319700; fax 01865 319701.

Web: Visit www.brf.org.uk

❑ Please do not send me further information about BRF publications.

GL0104